D0193119

Building an Ethical School

Building an Ethical School:
A Practical Response to the Moral Crisis in Schools

Robert J. Starratt

NATIONAL UNIVERSITY
LIBRARY   SAN DIEGO

The Falmer Press

(A member of the Taylor & Francis Group)
London • Washington, D.C.

UK   The Falmer Press, 4 John St, London WC1N 2ET
USA   The Falmer Press, Taylor & Francis Inc., 1900 Frost Road, Suite 101, Bristol, PA 19007

© Selection and editorial material copyright R. Starratt 1994

All rights reserved. No part of this publication may be reproduced, stored in a retrieval system, or transmitted, in any form or by any means, electronic, mechanical, photocopying, recording, or otherwise, without permission in writing from the Publisher.

First published 1994

A catalogue record of this publication is available from the British Library

ISBN 0 7507 0084 x cased
ISBN 0 7507 0085 8 paper

Library of Congress Cataloging-in-Publication Data are available on request

Jacket design by Caroline Archer

Typeset in 11/13 pt Bembo by
Graphicraft Typesetters Ltd., Hong Kong

Printed in Great Britain by Burgess Science Press, Basingstoke on paper which has a specified pH value on final paper manufacture of not less than 7.5 and is therefore 'acid free'.

Contents

List of Figures

Chapter 1

Building a What?

In a nearby school three eighth graders are overheard rehearsing 'today's problem with adults':

'What do they know about our kind of music anyway?'

'Yeah! You'd think they never had sex 'n' stuff in their own lives, the way they put down our music.'

'They can't *stand* having young people expressin' their own feelings. Like, we're just supposed to be like *them*.'

'Did you hear what Joey's parents did! They took his whole CD collection away from him. They go to one of those weird churches where they preach against kids' music.'

'Maria's parents won't let her go to the school dance, for cripes sakes. 'Fraid she'll get raped or somethin'. They told her the way kids dance is *suggestive*. What do they think dancin' is *supposed* to be, anyway!'

Whether the topic is sex or alcohol, or some other form of experimental recreation, youngsters talking among themselves tend to reject many norms of conventional ethical behavior. On the other hand, adults themselves are not altogether agreed on what should be allowed for other adults, let alone for children. Hence a proposal to engage in ethical education — to build a thoroughgoing school climate, culture, and program that promotes ethical learning — may appear to the optimist a bit risky, and to most, outright insanity.

In societies made up of diverse religious and cultural traditions, getting people to agree on the proper ethical response to a situation is difficult, and in some cases, impossible. In societies with strong traditions of separation between secular governments and religious bodies, there is an added fear that teaching moral and ethical values in state supported schools will necessarily involve the state in supporting a form of religious orthodoxy, or even simply in supporting belief in a transcendental being who rules the universe and who is the ground of all moral imperatives. Fearing the controversy and animosity which might result from attempting to promote an explicit ethical stand, school administrators and teachers tacitly and tactfully avoid ethical discussions.

Besides the concern that introducing ethics in schools would result in conflict and controversy among widely divergent ethical viewpoints, there is another concern felt by a smaller number of parents and educators. This concern is grounded in the belief that discussions about ethical issues do not belong in schools at all, but rather belong in homes and churches. Their argument is not based on the divisiveness issue. Rather, these people believe that there is a chasm between objective, scientific knowledge, and subjective ethical preferences and religious beliefs. In their minds, ethical principles are based on values, not on facts; ethics reflect cultural traditions, religious socialization, and personal preferences, not rigorous scientific proof; morality is somewhat like etiquette and social mores, acquired by socialization and example, not by logical argument. The importance of learning ethical behavior is not denied; the school is simply not the place to teach ethics. The school can teach obedience to laws and rules that guide public life, but there is no need to go into ethical reasons behind laws and rules. Even the legal profession no longer bothers with that.

Still others would have problems with the effort to build ethical schools, not so much on the grounds of avoiding controversy or because the teaching of ethics belongs in the home and with religious authorities, but on more pragmatic grounds: we simply do not have the time to give. Schools are already falling behind, many contend, in their primary job of teaching basic skills in language, science, and numeracy, let alone developing critical thinking skills for lifelong learning. There is talk of the need to increase the length of the school day and of the school year to improve *academic* achievement. If we are not getting the job done in academics, how can we afford to divert time and resources away from academics to attend to ethics?

There is yet another obstacle to building an ethical school, one that is both subtle, and, perhaps because it is rarely articulated, the most difficult to overcome. It is the growing indifference to the need for a common ethic. What used to be considered ethically objectionable is now acceptable, whether we are talking about casual sex, deceit in advertising, subtle forms of bribery of public officials, violations of contractual agreements, minor pilfering of company supplies, street violence, or illegal drug use. Driven by a relentless pursuit of material accumulation, recreational thrills, and a self-centered desire for power and status, more and more adults have accepted a privatized ethic of social Darwinism, where the individual is pitted against everyone else in an aggressive pursuit of self-interest. Normally this attitude is understated, rather than put in its more extreme forms: 'Look after yourself first, 'cause nobody else will'. 'That's simply the way business is done around here.' 'I'm not technically breaking the law, so what's the problem?' 'So it's against the law, but no one is getting hurt; look around you and see how many people are getting away with it.'

Those who hold these attitudes usually restrict their activities to minor ethical or legal infractions. They want to appear to be following the rules, after all. They have no concern, however, for holding their children to any ethical standard except the law of survival:

> Just teach the kids how to get good grades and test scores so they can get into a good college and get on with the real business of life. It's a dog-eat-dog world out there, and they have to learn how to compete in that world. Life will teach them the tough lessons of how to take care of themselves.

Finally, there are some who might support the need for ethical education, but are wary of attempting it because, in their minds, teachers are not competent to teach ethics. Few teachers in the schools have ever had a course in ethics. If we demand that teachers know mathematics or biology before teaching those subjects, how can we maintain a consistent demand for professional quality among our teachers when we ask them to attend to ethical concerns with no professional training in that area? Furthermore, teachers themselves exhibit the diversity of ethical positions found in public life on many important ethical issues. How can we expect the children to make sense out of people teaching them different ethical positions?

It might appear, then, that an effort to build an ethical school is doomed to failure at the outset. It is precisely because the task appears so daunting that this book has been written. The task promises challenges, no doubt about it, but the need to develop the ethical environment in schools is so great that we have to marshal the resources to bring it about. We will attempt answers to the above objections as the book unfolds, answers that indicate that the objections are not insurmountable. Indeed, we shall see that those objections do not stand up well to scrutiny. For now, we need to take stock of our present situation in schools and grasp the enormity of the task facing us. That task is no less than the task of reversing a massive deterioration in the ethical life of our society.

Facing the Problem

In the United States, information about increases in murder, rape, muggings, child abuse and other domestic violence, drug addiction, drug related crime, white-collar crime, corporate violation of tax, environmental, and price rigging laws is cumulatively depressing, if not terrifying. Children growing up in this kind of a society have to wonder whether the daily media reports of all of the above do not indicate that this kind of behavior is the norm, rather than the exception in human social living. Should they be blamed if, perceiving the world filled with these kinds of predators, they begin to espouse the ethic of the jungle, or, what may be worse, despair?

Besides the violence, depravity and deception found in public life, children and youth encounter appeals to the most self-indulgent, childish, manipulative and pornographic fantasies in the entertainment and advertising media. Children are exposed daily to television shows depicting violence, murder, and casual sex. They watch commercials in which sex is used to sell everything from beer to bath soap, from shaving cream to automobiles.

Parents do not always present uplifting ethical messages to youth. Rather, children see examples of cheating on taxes, getting parking tickets fixed, infidelities to the marriage bond, heavy drinking in the home, driving after heavy drinking, ethnic and racial jokes, occasional outbursts of physical violence in the home, deceitful and abusive language in the home, scapegoating and abusive labeling of people in the community. Unfortunately, they also encounter times when their own personal bond with the parent is fractured by anger, disinterest, manipulation, or even flagrant abuse.

Whether or not things are worse in the present day than in earlier times, the reporting of them brings the enormity of the problem to our awareness. However, with refinements in statistical record-keeping, we can be reasonably certain that a marked increase in the breakdown of ethical behavior in both the home and in public life over the past thirty years has occurred.

These statistics indicate that youth have been affected in this general breakdown. The incidence of murder, rape, drug abuse, theft, and physical violence among youth has increased dramatically over the past twenty years.[1] In both urban and suburban communities, child and adolescent sexual activity is almost taken for granted. What used to be considered abusive and vulgar scatological language can be heard among youngsters in the corridors of primary and middle schools, not to mention in comments to teachers. In many urban schools, students are required to pass through metal detector frames in order to enforce the prohibition against carrying guns and knives in school. Besides violence between gangs, we hear about youth harassing homeless people, or committing random acts of violence against those of another race. Most urban centers are awash in graffiti on buildings, buses and sidewalks, spray-painted there by young people. In several instances, a student on the way to or from school has been killed for not surrendering his or her sneakers or leather coat to a classmate. Among suburban high school students, drinking heavily throughout the weekend is a common practice, sometimes also involving drugs and sex.

The awareness that children and young people have always tested the limits of the boundaries adults established must be kept in perspective. Whether it was smoking behind the barn or using 'swear words', kids would get some thrill and satisfaction at doing something 'naughty' or trying out some kind of adult behavior. A certain amount of sexual experimentation has always gone on among children and adolescents. Kids lied to their parents, stayed out too late with their friends, had fights, bullied other kids, excluded other kids from their circle, made fun of handicapped people. To be sure, most adults can remember their youthful antics with a smile. Children are rarely 'good' for a whole day, let alone for a whole week. Reminding ourselves of that can help us avoid a kind of sanctimonious indignation over the actions of today's youth.

On the other hand, we have to look squarely at the real damage they are doing to themselves and to the community. Although some of their activities can be labeled as a harmless testing of limits, pranks and boisterous behavior, much of what we see now is vicious and destructive. What is worse is the assertion by some youngsters that adults have no *right* to tell them what they can and cannot do. It is the denial that there are *norms* that are being violated; they are responsible to community authorities and to principles of behavior that go beyond their whimsy or desire. As more and more young people grow up with a disregard for community standards of behavior, our society is in danger of descending into ethical anarchy.

Fortunately, there are signs that educators and parents are beginning to address the problem. We are finding more schools which have intentionally and programmatically begun to inculcate values of honesty, respect, responsibility and tolerance.[2] This book is intended for those educators and parents and school board/school council members who want to address the problem in a comprehensive way.

Response to Objectors

Let us suppose that we are sufficiently concerned about the problem of children and youth growing up with weak ethical foundations, how do we respond to the objections cited at the beginning of this chapter against the possibility of building an ethical school? Those objections are

1. in a pluralistic society, we cannot get agreement over which ethics to teach;
2. the teaching of ethics belongs in the family and the religious community, not in the school;
3. given the demands for time and resources to improve the academic performance of schools, we cannot take time and resources away from that primary task to channel into ethical education;
4. many parents no longer see any practical use for ethical education either in the home or in the school;
5. teachers cannot be involved in ethical education when they have had no preparation in it.

Let us try to answer those objections.

First of all, granted that we live in a pluralistic society, and that we value the diversity such pluralism lends to public life, we can nonetheless agree upon very basic values which schools should teach. Thomas Lickona argues for the two basic values of respect and responsibility.[3] Few people would argue that every person is entitled to a basic respect for his or her person, reputation and property. No one has the right to deny a person that basic respect. Likewise one should respect himself or herself. No one should heedlessly endanger her or his own life. Lickona extends this basic virtue of respect to the environment, that whole web of life that sustains us. This calls us to act sensitively toward our fragile ecosystem. Respect is the root principle behind many ethical 'don'ts'. Because we respect ourselves, other people and the environment we should not do X, Y and Z.

Responsibility emphasizes our positive obligations to care for each other. A sense of responsibility urges us to think of others, to help others in need, to honor a contract with another person, to be loyal and trustworthy. Whereas the virtue of respect counsels us not to engage in racial stereotyping, the virtue of responsibility counsels us to build community with all people. Not only am I obliged not to hurt someone; I am obliged to care for them. The question of how much I am obliged to care will always arise, and the general response is that I should care as much as I am able, even if that means only a smile or a gentle greeting. The responsibility ethic reminds us that it is not enough to avoid doing harm. We are obliged to do good.

Fox and DeMarco argue for three general moral principles which everyone is obliged to honor.[4] They are:

1 do no harm;
2 do not be unfair;
3 do not violate another's freedom.

Fox and DeMarco add to these general principles a 'prima facie restriction'.[5] The prima facie restriction means that other things being equal, the principle must be honored. When a principle is in conflict with another principle, or a particular case involves highly unusual circumstances, it may be overridden. However, the burden of proof is on the one requesting the exception. Thus, in the case of someone suffering an extremely painful irreversible illness, we are not obliged to use heroic or unusual measures to keep that person alive. But the burden of proof is on the person requesting the exemption to show that the illness is, under most circumstances, irreversible.

In speaking about their framing of the principles in negative statements, Fox and DeMarco indicate that negative statements tell us what we are bound to avoid doing. This does not imply that there are no positive obligations. With positive principles, such as the obligation to care for others, it is hard to determine when and how much they apply in particular cases. Thus, parents have a duty to care for their children, but other people are not obliged to care for them in the same way. However, all people are obliged not to harm them.

Thomas Green speaks of an education that nurtures conscience.[6] Although he conceives of conscience as unitary and personal, Green proposes that conscience has five voices: the call of craft, the call of membership, the call of sacrifice (or duty), the call of memory, and the call of imagination. A mature conscience calls us to integrity in our work (the call of craft). It reminds us that sloppy and careless work is undeserving of us and serves others poorly. It causes us to feel guilt or shame or embarrassment over a job poorly done, over careless attention to the simple things involved in conducting the business of everyday life.

The conscience of membership reminds us of our bonds and responsibilities to the community we belong to. By asserting the primacy of the community over the individual, Green emphasizes that education for a public life is the way, simultaneously, to form one's private conscience. Robert Coles, in a reflective insight bears this out. He recalls his father telling his brother and himself when they were young that 'character is how you behave when no one is looking'. Coles asks, however, 'Are we ever in a situation when no one is looking?' Coles argues that most morally conscientious people carry company inside them. They are, even when alone, in public.[7]

The third call of conscience, the conscience of sacrifice, calls us to go beyond self-interest. It is the desire to serve the good of others even at the cost of what one legitimately desires for oneself in the present. The keeping of promises or confidences, when not to do so would be to our advantage, is an example of the conscience of sacrifice. Parents who put aside their projects and plans in order to attend to the unexpected demands of their children respond to this call of conscience.

The fourth voice of conscience, the conscience of memory, is related to the conscience of membership. Through it we are rooted to and in the stories and traditions of our people and our place. The conscience of memory seems so poignantly illustrated in Richard Rodriguez's autobiography, *The Hunger of Memory*, in which he recounts his life-long struggle to be faithful to his Mexican heritage while trying to become a successful writer in the United States.[8]

The conscience of imagination, finally, allows us to claim solidarity with those who have been before us, to mourn their suffering and celebrate their humanity; to feel connected to other people we do not know personally; to feel responsibility for generations yet unborn. The call of imagination enables us to attend to people beyond our immediate community, even to those who may have been afflicted and oppressed by our way of life.

In later chapters we will go into the processes whereby a community chooses which ethical principles it will emphasize, or what kind of conscience it will form. For the moment it suffices to point out that even in the most diverse of communities, one can find agreement on basic ethical values. There may be differences in determining what specific behaviors constitute absolute violations of those values, or to what extent one is obliged in every case by those values, but they can agree on the value itself. Among some Americans, the value of patriotism is shown in supporting their country's foreign military interventions, whether or not they have serious reservations about them; other Americans, on the contrary, feel morally obliged by their patriotism to protest in public debate when they disagree with their country's military policies. Even in highly homogeneous communities, strong disagreements can arise about whether specific actions violate an ethical norm, even while they agree on the norm itself.

We can imagine, moreover, what a state of anarchy a society would be in if, due to divergences of values, they could not agree on any boundaries to social behavior. Life would be brought to a standstill while each individual argued for her or his right to do this or that, while others argued just as strenuously that they could not do this or that. Our life would degenerate into a total war of all against all. In the pluralistic society of the United States, we have ethical principles, the observance of which protects the very plurality that causes disagreements. Pluralism does not mean that we cannot, and in fact, do not agree on any number of principles which guide the way we conduct our lives. The nation was founded by leaders who held strong differences on many issues, but who also held other principles upon which they agreed and which came to define the parameters of public life. Any form of democracy will experience the tensions of diverse points of view; yet, there is the concomitant realization that there are bonds stronger than the fear of legal sanctions which urge the citizens to live cooperatively and in peace. These bonds are the values which people hold in common. Anthony Bryk puts it well:

> In writings as ancient as Aristotle and as contemporary as Gadamer, Habermas and Arendt, as secular as Dewey, and as religious as Aquinas, we find strong support for the contention that the survival of a pluralistic democracy requires a belief that mutual understanding among diverse parties can be achieved through genuine dialogue and critical encounter. The first moral principle of a democracy is the passionate commitment of its citizens to such a discourse.[9]

Bryk aptly connects this first moral principle of democracy with the corollary that moral education in a democracy's schools should stimulate in students a vision of what democracy can be and nurture those habits of both the heart and the mind that will sustain them in the pursuit of that vision.[10]

To those who object that ethics should be taught at home and in church, but not at school there are several answers. First, the absolute separation between fact and value is a proposition which recent scientists and philosophers have called increasingly into question.[11] Originally proposed by scientists and philosophers as a way to protect the objectivity and purity of the scientific ways of knowing from more subjective assertions of preference, poetry or philosophical speculation, this separation of fact from value has come to be seen as specious. Scientific facts take on meaning and significance in a network of ideas and assumptions which scientists make, which themselves have not been subjected to scientific proof. Furthermore, ever since Kuhn's publication of *The Structure of Scientific Revolutions*, the creative and imaginative side of scientific theory and research has been seen as equally important to the progress of science as the rigorous attention to detail and measurement.[12] Furthermore, throughout the history of science, scientists have been influenced in their work by both noble and ignoble values. Science, moreover, is no longer seen as the only legitimate form of knowledge. Practical and aesthetic knowledge, as well as moral inquiry are seen as having a legitimacy of their own. Hence the argument to deny ethics a legitimate place in schools on the grounds that it is not scientific is based on false, and presently discredited, assumptions.

Furthermore, to argue that ethics is purely a matter of subjective choice or preference, or a matter relegated to religious beliefs and dogma is also misguided. Ethics can be and has been the subject of public debate and public consensus. As early as the time of Aristotle, ethics has been seen as a public concern of the community. Aristotle called ethics a kind of practical knowledge, a knowledge which was gained by living in the community and experiencing the life of the community in all its richness and complexity.[13] Ethical understanding was gained from reflecting on the ways the community solved the practical problems of living together in a self-governing community. In one sense, ethical knowledge did not issue in absolutes, for the community never came up with the one best way to respond in all situations. Nevertheless one learned how to be an ethical person by living in the community and learning the normal ways the community conducted its affairs and relationships.

Hence it is a narrow view of ethics which would constrain it to subjective individual choice, or to principles derived from religious dogma. Ethics are concerned with the public life of the community. This is not to say that the home and the religious authorities do not play important parts in the inculcating of ethical values. Parents have the primary obligation to teach their children the basic norms of social living. The religious community has the right to teach the ethical components of its religious traditions. In those circumstances where the home, the religious community and the school stand clearly for the same ethical norms, youngsters tend to reflect those norms very consistently. From the founders of the United States to the present, however, there has been a strong tradition of belief that a strong democracy required schools in which ethical behavior was stressed.[14] Schools were not seen as opposing religious community or home in the teaching of ethics. Rather, schools were seen as complementing them, especially in those ethical matters that concerned public life in a democracy, where individuals encountered the demands of civil self-government. Precisely because the United States was made up of peoples from different religious and cultural traditions, schools were to be the places where youngsters learned a common ethic, an ethic which would bind them together, despite their diverse backgrounds.

Because the early efforts to instill virtue in children and youth was tied so closely to religion, as the schools became less under the influence of religious bodies, much of the explicitly religious foundations for ethical behavior were bleached out of the curriculum and general discipline of school life. As more and more Supreme Court decisions about religion in the schools were decided on the Constitutional doctrine of the separation of church and state, public or state schools withdrew much of the explicitly ethical components from their curriculum. Textbooks removed much of their moralizing tone. Hence, the schools themselves seemed unsure of how to teach an ethic which did not require an explicitly religious foundation. The question facing many schools is precisely this: granting that many people in the community agree that we should teach ethics, how can we do this without a foundation in religion? The question is not so much whether to have ethical schools; rather, the question is how do we do it within state and federal laws?[15]

Then there is the practical objection that, given a limited school day and school budget already inadequate to achieve our academic goals, how can we siphon off resources for the effort to teach ethics? It is the demand to do more with less. First of all, schools are already teaching ethics. It is impossible to run an ethically neutral school. Day in and day out students are picking up ethical influences, whether it be the example of the adults and peers in the schools, the way the school handles discipline, the implied moral lessons in much of the curriculum, the ethical lessons learned on the playing field and in other extracurricular activities. Obviously schools could do a better job with more time, more professional staff, more resources. Lacking these, schools simply have to improve the quality of the ethical lessons students experience in the regular school day. (Examples of schools who have done it are in Appendix I.) A lot has to do with attention to the small details, and with an institutional consistency in promoting agreed upon values. Rather than add on new courses in ethics, teachers can make use of an abundance of ethically pregnant material already in the curriculum that has not been attended to. It is not a question of working longer hours; it is a question of working smarter, of improving the quality of all the human interactions now taking place in the normal school day.

The fourth objection to building an ethical school is offered by those parents for whom ethics is obsolete, impractical, not even a consideration when it comes to getting by in the world. My response is simply this. Look around you. Do we want to surrender our public life to the growing anarchy we see every day, not only in our cities, but in the suburbs as well? Or do we need to reassess what has amounted to our abdication of responsibility as adults to set limits to what is publicly allowable? My response to these parents is that the disintegration of public life has reached intolerable limits. It has reached its present state of disarray because a significant proportion of adults in society turned away from their responsibility to teach their children what was acceptable and not acceptable behavior, based on some concern for the common good. Many parents thought that it was not healthy to restrict freedom of expression and freedom of action. Having loosened the reins of behavior in the interests of individual freedom, however, we have arrived at the point where we can understand that individual freedom has to be balanced against responsibility to and for the common good of the community. Few, if any, societies have ever achieved a perfect balance between individual freedoms and community obligations, but surely ours is seriously unbalanced at present.

A school community which wants to build an ethical school must confront the apathy and indifference of parents and challenge them to get involved. Both the parents and the teachers will have to explore ways to get these indifferent parents involved, for parental involvement is the most important component in building an ethical school. As we will see in succeeding chapters, there are ways to foster such involvement.

Finally, in response to the objection that teachers have no formal training in ethics and therefore are unable to teach ethics, we respond in two ways. First, teachers are already teaching ethical behavior and attitudes both by their example and in the multitudinous informal ways they interact with children and youth. Are they doing it well? In most cases, yes. Are they experts? Probably not. But ask the children whether the teachers taught them much about being good people, and they will point to numerous instances when this or that teacher taught them a valuable lesson. Second, we are talking more about a lot of common-sense ethical education. We do not expect teachers to become professional ethicians.

Most teachers were never trained in how to use computers in their teaching. They learned on the job. They went to seminars and workshops and taught one another. In building an ethical school we must obviously attend to the professional growth of teachers in their facility to engage in ethical education. It would be ridiculous to hand teachers a new program for ethics education on the first day of school and expect them to implement it. In the process of designing and planning for an ethical school, teachers will need to be involved in the discussions and in some specialized training, but it will not be very esoteric stuff. To the objectors we say thank you for reminding us to attend to the training of teachers. We intend that to become an intrinsic part of the process of building an ethical school.

If we agree that there is a pressing need for greater attention to ethical education, and if we agree that the objections to trying it are not insurmountable, then where do we begin? I suggest that we take a look at some of the underlying frames of mind encountered both in school and in the culture which make ethical growth problematic for youngsters. That may enable us to chart a general course. Then, it seems, we ought to consider those values which constitute a rock-bottom foundation for ethical education. Are there basic human qualities that are a prerequisite for any kind of ethical action? After exploring some possible foundational qualities, we might then take a look at some of the schools of thought currently dealing with ethical education to see whether they point us in some promising directions. Can we come up with some overarching frameworks that encompass the helpful insights of ethical theories, despite their differences?

Assuming we can get that far, we would then want to consider what a comprehensive plan for an ethical school might look like. By reviewing such a plan we might see some concrete possibilities for our school. Next we will need to think about a process of involving people in discussing the need for and possibilities of an ethical school. Various constituencies will need to be involved, since the effort will require a broad base of support and commitment. Some tentative process should be mapped out in the beginning so that groups will have a sense of what their involvement will entail. These procedural plans can be modified once the group settles into the work. Some exploration of design features and support structures for various possible models of ethical schools should be considered ahead of time so as to be able to prime the pump for the working groups. All of these elements will be taken up in succeeding chapters.

Notes

1   *Age-Specific Arrest Rates and Race-Specific Arrest Rates for Selected Offenses, 1965–1988* (1990) Washington, DC, FBI.

2   See the many examples cited in Lickona, T. (1991) *Educating For Character*, New York, Bantam Books.
3   Lickona (1991) pp. 43–45.
4   Fox, R.M. and DeMarco, J.S. (1990) *Moral Reasoning*, Fort Worth, TX, Holt, Rinehart and Winston.
5   Fox and DeMarco (1990) pp. 170–2.
6   Green, T.F. (1985) 'The formation of conscience in an age of technology', *American Journal of Education*, 93, pp. 1–38.
7   Coles, R. (1989) *The Call of Stories*, Boston, Houghton-Mifflin, p. 198.
8   Rodriguez, R. (1981) *Hunger of Memory*, Boston, David R. Godine.
9   Bryk, A.S. (1988) 'Musings on the moral life of schools', *American Journal of Education*, 96, p. 259.
10 Bryk (1988) pp. 261–2.
11 See the well reasoned essay by Bruce Jennings, 'Interpretive social science and policy analysis', in Callahan, D. and Jennings, B. (Eds) (1983) *Ethics, The Social Sciences, and Policy Analysis*, New York, Plenum Press, pp. 3–35.
12 Kuhn, T.S. (1962) *The Structure of Scientific Revolutions*, Chicago, The University of Chicago Press.
13 Aristotle, *Nicomachean Ethics*, Book VI.
14 See Neufeldt, H.G. (1981) 'Religion, morality and schooling: Forging the nineteenth century Protestant consensus', in Hunt T.C. and Maxson, M.M. (Eds) *Religion and Morality in American Schooling*, Washington, DC, University Press of America, pp. 3–29; Tyack, D. (1967) *Turning Points in American Educational History*, New York, John Wiley & Sons, pp. 83–118.
15 For an ongoing effort to reconstruct this traditional concern for ethical education, see the work of James Fowler in the Project on Ethics and Public Education. Fowler works out of the Center for Faith Development of Emory University in Atlanta, Georgia. A summary of the work in progress can be found in Fowler, J. (1990) 'Reconstructing Paideia in public education', in Palmer, P.J., Wheeler, B.G. and Fowler, J. (Eds) *Caring for the Commonweal: Education for Religious and Public Life*, Macon, GA, Mercer University Press, pp. 63–89.

Chapter 2

Moral Problematics in Schools

Because the situations of schooling are in flux, especially in the present ground swell of school reform, it is difficult to present a picture of the moral problematics of schools which fits all schools. Moreover, schools are very complex environments. To try to understand what is *really* going on in any one school is next to impossible, because so much is going on simultaneously. On any given day teachers will be brilliant and insensitive within the same class period; administrators will simultaneously offend some parents and please others by the announcement of a new student regulation; a student will be inventive, contrary, mean and thoughtful — all during a thirty minute lunch period. Throughout the day students hear conflicting value messages urging both creativity and conformity, individuality and community, competition and cooperation, equality and social Darwinism. These messages are interwoven into an unpredictable and freely adjusting ethical tapestry throughout classrooms, gymnasium, playground, and principal's office. Moreover, they are received by youngsters whose varying cultural and class backgrounds filter these messages in positive and negative colorations.

Some studies of schools and classrooms point out the everyday ebb and flow of affection and anger, teasing and taunting, enthusiasm and evasion, brilliance and dullness between teachers and students.[1] Other studies attempt to point out the underlying regularities that endure throughout the school year, patterns of teaching and organization which tend to leave a more consistent impression on students. Robert Dreeben's *On What is Learned in School*, Nancy Lesko's *Symbolizing Society*. Sarah Lightfoot's *The Good High School*, and John Goodlad's *A Place Called School* are examples of such studies.[2] One might be able to point to a teacher, to a student, or to a school activity which did not conform to the patterns and regularities observed in these studies.

Nonetheless, the large patterns and regularities tend to influence and impact the majority of the students.

I would like to suggest some patterns of thinking and acting in schools which are ethically problematic in their influence, both real and potential, on children and youth. In offering these generalities, and perhaps even exaggerating them in order to make a point, I realize that these do not apply to all schools, nor to all students and teachers in every school. Nevertheless, these generalities suggest collectively that the schools are tilted too much in one direction toward certain values, and that this tilt ignores competing values which, if attended to, would provide a more balanced value foundation for ethical education. In brief, I suggest that the schools are tilted too much toward individualism, toward competition, toward a superficial form of rationality, toward privatism and individual achievement, and toward conformity to authority. After describing these failings, I will point out what competing values they ignore and suggest that a more balanced value foundation can enable the building of an ethical school.

Individualism

Statements of school philosophies and school-wide goals almost always center on the growth of the individual — growth of the student's intellectual, social, physical and emotional well-being. In classrooms the focus is on the progress of the individual student. It appears unthinkable that an individual's progress could be subordinated to the progress of the group. In the minds of most educators, the group is simply the collection of the individuals in the group, not an entity whose achievement might have a special significance. Suggesting that the attitudes and practices of the group could collectively have a qualitatively significant impact on the achievement of the individual, and that group activity might in some instances be more desirable than individual striving would encounter strong resistance from some educators and parents.

Attending to within-group problems in the classroom, problems such as stereotyping and scapegoating, racial, sexual and ethnic antagonisms could have an effect on the quality of learning in a class. Over the course of a year, this might make a considerable difference in the achievement of all individuals in the class. School-wide attention to such problems could also promote the learning readiness and general academic attitudes of many students who frequently feel that the school does not support or respect them.[3] Yet many schools are run as though the social climate of the classroom and the school have nothing to do with the quality of students' academic achievement. Individual students pass or fail, not families, not teams of students, not whole classrooms, not, certainly, the school. Learning achievement in school implies no responsibility to anyone else in the school. If students fail, it is their own fault. Even if the school culture tends to favor males who come from white, upper middle-class backgrounds, anyone who fails has only herself or himself to blame.

In many schools the message is:

> You are on your own. You make it on your own; you mess up on your own. You have to take responsibility for number one, and number one only. Being nice to other people is an add-on, a pleasant bonus. But the real business at hand is getting all you can get for yourself, because everyone else is out to get as much as they can for themselves. Don't expect your peers to step aside and let you pass; don't expect your peers to stop or delay their advance in order to pick you up when you stumble. Being in the top fifty percent of the class means that you stand above fifty percent of your peers. You can't have 100 percent of the class in the top fifty percent of the class. Those in the bottom fifty percent are there because they didn't work hard enough. It is their fault.

Even if every student was bright and worked to his or her absolute maximum, there would still be a bottom 50 percent. Our society cannot yet tolerate a whole graduation class of valedictorians, where everyone achieved a perfect score. Somehow or other, that school would be considered too easy. Yet we have sports teams which are considered champions. Collectively they achieve a standard of excellence, even though every person on the team contributes something unique and special. What is wrong with a school as a learning community achieving collectively a standard of excellence, even though individuals contribute to that excellence using different talents and passions?

Simply to suggest this arrangement goes against the grain of how we expect schools to be run. Schools are run on the assumption that, when it comes to rationality and intelligence, the individual is the source, not the group or the community. This belief expresses a deeply held conviction and value about the individual as the basic social unit, as a self-determining agent, and as the source of his or her own ideas. This belief affirms that the individual's achievement is where the merit lies; that is what should be rewarded.

Outside of schools, we seem far more sensible about this rigid individuality. Commercial enterprises reflect a more generous view of the individual as a member of a team, of a collective effort. One of the exciting developments in business is the formation of project teams to solve problems, design new products, explore new marketing strategies. Instead of having individuals working in isolation on highly specific tasks, business corporations have learned the value of teams of workers sharing ideas and imaginings for the improvement of their work.

From a more profoundly philosophical viewpoint, we also realize that tradition and culture provide the ongoing pool of ideas, mores, frameworks, even language, for individuals within any community to think, perceive and express themselves.[4] The community and its traditions are the source of all the taken-for-granted certainties of the individual, including the correct names for things. The individual is embedded in the culture and its traditions. Even to reject a particular piece of what the culture affirms as true, the individual has to use all the tools and understandings which the culture makes available in order to argue his or her case. In other words, the individual is not the isolated, autonomous being supposed in classical liberal theory, but a social–cultural being who is both an individual and a reflector of the culture of the community. Tradition is both the gift with which the individual creates his or her individuality and against which he or she fights in order not to be submerged as a non-individual.[5]

Competition

Closely tied to the emphasis on individualism is the emphasis on competition. Students are pitted against one another for their rank in class and on test score rankings. When the valedictorian of the class wins out over her or his rivals by one one-thousandth of a point, then every single grade on every single assignment counts in that kind of competition. Besides competing against one another for the limited rewards within the school, students are also competing against faceless unknown others from other schools in the city or the region or the country for scarce seats in the better colleges and universities. Parents often bring enormous pressures to bear on their children to achieve, not so much for what intrinsically worthwhile things they might learn, but more for the accumulation of high grades on their transcripts, which in turn get translated into class rank. High grades are the chits which can be traded in for entry to prestigious institutions of higher education.

In the educational reform literature, so called public-spirited leaders in government and commerce have spoken and continue to speak about the schools' role in keeping the country competitive in global markets. Teachers pick up that rhetoric and pass it along to the students. Hence competition becomes almost a way of life. Compete for grades; compete for colleges, compete for jobs, compete for power, compete for the country. There is a popular argument that by creating national academic standards, the national curriculum to enable students to meet those standards, pedagogies which will 'deliver' such a curriculum, and tests to measure student progress, we will return to the leadership of world markets.

There is ample evidence that this reasoning is simply wrong. After the Second World War, the United States was the only industrialized nation that had not suffered crippling damage to its infrastructure. Its factories were intact and highly productive. It was easy for the US to dominate world trade while others were in the early stages of recovery. Since that time European and Asian nations have rebuilt themselves, and the competition is now more vigorous. Furthermore, Third World nations have also industrialized and have joined the competition, often without the overhead costs of and concern for worker safety and environmental protection. Furthermore, the failure of American businesses to modernize and to devote a realistic percentage of their budgets to research and development was not due to declining test scores in American schools. Neither were American schools to blame for the political failures of government to control the growth of the national debt or to rein in the recklessness of bankers and investors which caused widespread bankruptcies and the dismantling of quality businesses through corporate takeovers. Clearly there is room for improvement in American schools, but their contribution to the decline of the US economy has been exaggerated beyond all proportion.

To return to the theme of competition, I would wager that, despite the rhetoric of academic competition, most students do not take it seriously because the rewards are not significant to them. Parents make a big fuss over grades. Because it may mean the withdrawal of privileges at home (watching an extra hour of television, having to come in early at night, loss of the car, etc.), students will get good enough grades to please their parents and avoid being brow-beaten. Because the school can also punish a poor performance by withholding eligibility in athletics and other activities, as well as promotion and graduation, most students will do well enough to avoid a failing grade. By and large, however, they do not find studying their school subjects intrinsically rewarding enough to make a consistent, high quality effort. Furthermore, the youth culture on the whole disparages getting high grades and cooperating with adult authority figures.

Hence, the competition ethic, while influencing the design of curriculum, class assignments, testing and pedagogy, does not affect student motivation. Those who do work hard and strive to achieve are rarely driven by the desire to excel *against others*. Rather, there seem to be other motives at play, such as the desire to excel for its own sake — simply to get the A, no matter how many others do or do not get it. Among a small minority of students, there is intrinsic intellectual and personal satisfaction in the studies. Among others there is the desire to get good grades in order to get ahead, to get into a good college and to get a good job, without necessarily finding anything intrinsically rewarding about academic work.

Nevertheless, if the curriculum and the teaching and the pedagogy is set up so as to encourage competition among students for grades, that will affect the kind of learning opportunities students experience. Basically they will be encouraged to study on their own, to do their homework on their own, and they will be tested as independent learners. In other words, the competition ethic goes hand and hand with the individualism cited above. Although one might cite the growing trend in cooperative arrangements for learning, group performance tests, and peer instruction, these trends eventually succumb to the competition and individualism ethic.

Superficial Forms of Rationality

Studies of classroom teaching indicate that in the large majority of classrooms only a superficial mastery of the subject matter is required, a mastery based primarily on memorization of definitions and information.[6] Rarely are students asked to question and critique information, or to assemble information into argument and exposition. Standardized testing reinforces this classroom emphasis on memory through the format of multiple-choice questions. Information in such tests is treated as isolated bits of 'right answers'. Usually these right answers have little or no connection to important questions which deal with the larger pattern of relationships among the bits of information, questions which require higher order thinking, weighing of conflicting evidence, judgments of taste or diplomacy.[7]

I am not arguing for the neglect of memory in the process of learning. There are a large number of facts, definitions, formulas, theorems, hypotheses, and even whole literary, philosophical and legal passages which need and ought to be committed to memory. I would agree with Hirsch and others that there is a floor of cultural literacy that requires knowledge of basic information about our traditions and cultural past.[8] It is also true that much of the classical heritage in literature, history and science provides ample opportunity for raising basic questions about human nature, the meaning of virtue, the forms of society, interpretations of justice, so that in the process of being exposed to the treasures of our cultural heritage, one also might be tempted to think about the large issues with which they dealt. Yet the realities of schooling — the fragmentation of the school day by attention to six, seven or eight distinct 'subjects', the frequent quizzes and tests which seek for simple recall of isolated bits of knowledge, the pressure on the teacher to cover a prescribed syllabus, and the failure to connect the subject matter of the classroom to the life-worlds of children and youth — tend to leave little room for attention to these more complex and more profound kinds of learning.

Hence what passes for rational activity in schools is predominantly superficial. Since there is little or no effort on the part of adults to connect what is learned in school with students' experience, or with the 'real world', rationality gradually takes on a meaning for youngsters as something equated with being clever, or with memorization of information, with applying the model problem to academic questions to find the 'right' answer. Rationality tends not to be something one develops as a way to gain clarity about one's life, about what is real and what is phony in social and political relations. The life of the mind is not cultivated with a passion to discover meaning and significance in history or literature or the arts. There is little sense in school that school lessons might involve weighty issues of life and death, joy and tragedy, no sense that the struggle to be a somebody in life requires disciplined reflection and a concentration on intelligible principles. Rather, what is communicated is an instrumental use of one's intelligence to get grades, to figure out the answers someone else wants to questions that someone else has posed. Why? Simply to get ahead. It is called achievement. But what is achieved beyond the grades and the class rank, and the promotion to the next grade, and, eventually, the diploma?

Schools tend to reduce rationality to skills, to the processing of information and the repackaging of information, but always to satisfy some external criteria of 'achievement' defined by some impersonal other, an organization, a government agency, a commercial enterprise. The more that students accept this practical definition of intelligence, the less they feel any responsibility for what they know.

The longer schools ignore the connections between school learnings and personal experience, the greater the chasm between students' personal and private meanings and their sense of the public realm as a place where one engages information in order to commodify it in a quest to achieve.

At the end of every major lesson, unit, project or chapter, after they have been tested for a basic grasp of the material, students should be asked to respond to two further questions: 'What does this mean to you?' 'What does this mean for you, personally?' The first question implies that the student can give several illustrations, citing examples from aspects of life familiar to him or her, of what the material means. Answers to this question would often involve metaphor, simile, comparisons and contrasts, as well as the drawing of relationships. Answers to the second question would involve explorations of consequences in one's own life and in one's community. What does Shakespeare's *Romeo and Juliet* mean to you? for you? What does the principle of gravity mean to you? for you? What does the principle of supply and demand mean to you? for you? What does freedom of speech mean to you? for you? What does the Civil War mean to you? for you? What does Van Gogh's *Sunflowers* mean to you? for you? What does this photograph you took for your assignment mean to you? for you?

Those two questions force students to relate what they are involved with in class to their sense of the larger world and of their own lives, their sense of themselves. Those questions force them to consider relationships and connections among ideas and experiences. They often force students to reflect on personal values and social value systems. They occasionally force them to be critical of themselves and of their community. Those questions habituate them to seeing that knowledge should lead to understanding, to forming interpretive perspectives on various aspects of life, to the posing of new questions, to appreciating things and people in their own right, to forming opinions, grounding beliefs, expressing the poetry, the harmony, the pathos, the music embedded in reality. If knowledge is presented as divorced from value and from a moral quest, then students come to view knowledge simply as a neutral coinage of exchange, rather than as a precious heritage, a linkage to practical and useful action, a valued achievement after a difficult struggle, a beautifully crafted understanding.[9]

Such an instrumentalizing of knowledge and rationality is not confined to schools. Indeed the exclusive use of calculated intelligence to achieve instrumental ends without reference to substantive purpose and value has been criticized as one of the tragic flaws of the modern world, a world that can build ever more sophisticated instruments of war, but cannot figure out when and if waging a war is moral.[10] In other words, the modern world often seems to lose sight of the moral and human purposes to be served by its technological and administrative advances. It has become fascinated with *techne*, the unending production of successive generations of inventions: computers, telecommunication systems, satellites, space machines, diagnostic medical machinery, gene splicing, atom smashing, microwave cooking — the list goes on and on. Instrumental rationality involves the drive for ever more efficient ways of production. Efficiency, when it becomes the primary value, tends to ignore human concerns; it tends to treat human beings as means to an end, the ends of greater profits, lower production costs, speed of production. When instrumental rationality is not grounded in substantive rationality — that rationality which probes human meaning and human purposes — then it has no moral base. Often this leads to the irony of human inventions enslaving humans, whether that invention be an economic system, a political ideology, gambling, alcohol or a grading system.

Privatism and Individual Achievement

Because schools tend to create a protective wall between themselves and the outside world, they create an unreal inner world within the school. The school's curriculum tends to be self-justifying and self-explaining. That is, it is not related to the larger social and political world of public policy, commercial enterprise, political struggle and human tragedy. History books do not expose youngsters to the shocking details of brutality, betrayal, terror and disease that have ravaged past societies; there is little or no treatment of the cynicism of statesmen, the stupidity of monarchs, the reckless violence of mobs, the terrible agony of humans consumed by napalm, the stench of the madhouse or the cruelty of the prison. History is sanitized by the textbook industry and by teachers. Economics is taught as a rational science, not as a struggle of greed, envy, power, egoism, manipulation, deceit, exploitation, blackmail and subtle violence, rationalized by 'principles of the market'. In literature and art classes textbooks and library collections are censored in various subtle and overt ways so that youngsters are exposed only to the more virtuous models of human behavior. This censorship of intrusions from the real world is carried on in everyday teaching: there is no mention of the present condition of the state or the community, no questions raised about new laws, about the winners and losers in local referenda, no discussion of current issues highlighted in the newspaper. Youngsters are encouraged to go about their work and their play as though their work and their lives had no connection with the larger realities of the world outside the walls of the school. They have their lessons to learn, their games to play, their rules to keep. How to make sense of the larger world seems not to be included in the school's goals and objectives.

The large message conveyed by this separation from the real world is that the most important reality is a private reality, which includes the collective private reality of the school. Linked with the stress on individualism, the privatization of reality leads youngsters to think only of themselves and their immediate friends. They seem to have no obligations to the larger society except to obey certain rules and laws, like observing traffic signals and not stealing candy in the shopping mall. Their experience within school throughout their first sixteen to eighteen years is a privatized focus on themselves and their school work and their school activities. It's as though they are at the center of the universe, as though that whole world out there continues to spin on its own, providing them with food and clothing and video cassettes and music and cars and trains and airplanes and telephones. They can live in their private cocoon without any sense of responsibility to that 'outside' world, without any sense of people suffering and in pain, of people who are afraid and alienated, without any sense that that world is in danger of economic or environmental collapse, without feeling needed by that world, without any sense that the multiple human gifts they possess are owed to that world.

Conformity to Authority

The goals to be achieved, whether academic or extra-curricular, are almost always dictated by adults in authority. The curriculum to be mastered, whether a body of knowledge, the skill of correct grammatical expression, or the techniques of debate, are usually predetermined by the authorities. Assignments are to be uniformly completed according to prearranged formats; classroom protocols for asking questions are to be followed; behavior in the corridors and in the school yard is monitored and controlled.

In other words, students' activities are tightly controlled and channelled. Obedience and conformity are required. There may be some room for creativity and spontaneity, but the boundaries are defined by those in authority who enjoy unquestioned rights to reward and punish. A student who experiences this type of control year after year in school is socialized into a culture of conformity, and a learned dependency for one's sense of self-worth on the approval of those in authority.

Where little self-expression is allowed, where the exploration of alternative choices and the discovery of their consequences are blocked, there can be little growth in autonomy and in an internal sense of responsibility for one's choices. Impulse control may be necessary from time to time in the education of all students, especially the younger ones. When control is the only agenda of adults in authority, however, the development of a mature ethical person who acts with a sense of responsibility toward others at the same time as pursuing legitimate attempts at self-expression and authentic interaction with the natural and social world is thwarted. It leaves the person dependent on those in authority to define in every case what is right and wrong. It disposes the young toward passive acceptance of authority rather than active cooperation with those in authority in pursuit of a clearly desirable social good.

Furthermore, that large external world out there seems to get along just fine without their participation in its governance. They are not needed to solve its problems or improve its quality of life. No one in that larger world seems to take them seriously — at least no one has come into the school to ask their help, to ask their advice, to ask them to think about a problem the world faces.

In other words, youngsters derive no sense of meaning or purpose from the possibility of being involved in their larger world. Being protected from its pain and struggle, from its goodness and its evil, there are no large lessons to be learned about what it means to be a human being. Since they are not needed their experience of life is narrowed down to what happens in the private sphere — their games, their entertainments, their school work, their small joys and grievances within their circle of friends. Life becomes defined as what happens to me. Fulfillment is defined within my private world. Morality is defined by the small obligations I incur in this private world.

However, there is an insistent message which intrudes upon this private world: achievement. Youngsters are taught that their self-worth is tied up in achievement. They have to do something which measures up to someone else's criteria for achievement. Normally that means achieving high or passing grades. That is supplemented by involvement in school activities. One achieves by making the cheerleading squad or the basketball team, or by being elected to student government (although what one is supposed to achieve once elected to student government is carefully, though ambiguously, circumscribed within certain expressive activities).

Youngsters are taught to have goals, achievable goals. Achieving one's goals usually results in an award, like a trophy, a school letter, an emblem, a pin or a hat. While motivating youngsters to reach beyond complacency for some ambitious goals is usually healthy, it can also become an obsession. The often criticized American compulsion to activity, summarized in the statement, 'Don't just stand there, *do* something!' can be seen in an overemphasis on achievement. The youngster who likes to browse in the library, listen to music, think about a question, get lost in observing wildlife — 'school people' have problems with them. They seem not to be adequately focused on their work. They seem to be wasting time.

Besides slighting the more contemplative enjoyments of human experience, the stress on achievement can also lead to a neglect of many quality-of-life issues, and among them moral issues. We all know of the athletes whose drive to achieve led them to cut corners, or to endanger the lives of their teammates. The newspapers carry stories of people (usually men) whose ambition to achieve fame, fortune, power, political office, led them into illegal and unethical actions. The drive to achievement can be a very selfish and self-centered kind of activity. Achievement should be placed alongside other obligations and other worthwhile social activities. Youngsters can be so badgered into achieving that they never have time for good conversation, for recreational reading, for family and friends.

The above descriptions of the moral problematics in today's schools are basically about middle-class schools, not inner-city schools serving poor, minority communities. Inner-city schools can themselves be so impoverished as to make all discussions of them becoming ethical environments a farce. Jonathan Kozol's description of such schools in *Savage Inequalities* is a stark testimony of an unethical practice within the civic communities where these schools are to be found.[11] The schools themselves could not propose to teach ethics to children; the very condition of the buildings and the lack of basic resources speak of a system of injustice and prejudice which blatantly contradicts a concern for human dignity upon which an ethical education might be built.

What ethics the children of the minority underclass learn is learned from heroic parents who refuse to allow the welfare system and the chaos of their neighborhoods to defeat them. Or it is learned from an influential teacher who continues to care for them despite the obvious neglect of the school authorities. Or it is learned by happenstance in the neighborhood, from a coach, a case worker, some friends, the example of older youth. But often what ethical education takes place in urban neighborhoods is the ethics of survival of the fittest, or simply the ethics of getting by.

Summary

Further reflection may illuminate other patterns of school life that militate against a concern for nurturing ethical dispositions and attitudes. The ones I have mentioned here tend to militate against the experience of belonging to a community and of obligations to one's fellows, against a focus on deeper human purposes and values, against a sense of social responsibility and participation in civic governance, and against the general moral involvement with satisfying human relationships. It is important to reflect on the moral problematics embedded in the life of the school before launching on a formal effort at building an ethical school, because inattention to these often unseen problems can vitiate the more formal programs we might initiate.

Discussions among faculty, students and parents can help to expose the particular expressions of these problematics in the school. These discussions would lead to minor and major adjustments in the way the school conducts its business that itself might lead to an awareness of competing values. Yet, the school community might continue to muddle through its collective effort to be ethical, without any clear sense of a foundation upon which they might build a more comprehensive effort, or without any clear notions of a core of ethical values to guide its practical decisions. To those concerns we now turn our attention in the next two chapters.

Notes

1 See Kohl, H. (1967) *36 Children*, New York, The New American Library; Lopate, P. (1975) *Being With Children*, New York, Poseidon Press; Mathews, J. (1988) *Escalante: The Best Teacher in America*, New York, Henry Holt; Kidder, T. (1989) *Among Schoolchildren*, New York, Avon Books.

2 Dreeben, R. (1968) *On What is Learned in School*, Reading, MA, Addison Wesley; Lightfoot, S. (1983) *The Good High School: Portraits of Character and Culture*, New York, Basic Books; Goodlad, J.I. (1984) *A Place Called School*, New York, McGraw-Hill; Lesko, N. (1988) *Symbolizing Society*, London, Falmer Press.

3 See Joseph Murphy and Philip Hallinger's (1989) insightful study,

'Equity and access to learning: Curricular and instructional differences', *Journal of Curriculum Studies*, **21**, 3, pp. 120–34.

4 See Shils, E. (1981) *Tradition*, Chicago, University of Chicago Press; Bowers, C.A. (1987) *Toward a Post-Liberal Theory of Education*, New York, Teachers College Press.

5 See the telling arguments summarized by Bowers (1987) pp. 53–78.

6 Goodlad, J.I. (1984) *A Place Called School: Prospects for the Future*, New York, McGraw-Hill; Sedlak, M.W., Wheeler, C.W., Pullin, D.C. and Cusick, P.A. (1986) *Selling Students Short: Classroom Bargains and Academic Reform in American High Schools*, New York, Teachers College Press.

7 McNeil, L.M. (1986) *Contradiction of Control: School Structure and School Knowledge*, London, Routledge and Kegan Paul.

8 Hirsch, E.D., Jr. (1987) *Cultural Literacy*, Boston, Houghton Mifflin. I would argue that Hirsh's required curriculum is too narrow, but he does have a point.

9 For an expanded statement on the multidimensionality of knowledge, see Starratt, R.J. (1989) 'Knowing at the level of sympathy: A curriculum challenge', *Journal of Curriculum and Supervision*, **4**, 3.

10 See the extensive critique offered by Jurgen Habermas (1971) in *Knowledge and Human Interests* (trans. by J. Shapiro) Boston, Beacon Press. For a more thoroughgoing critique of the instrumental rationality of the curriculum, see Popkowitz, T. (1991) *A Political Sociology of Educational Reform*, New York, Teachers College Press.

11 Kozol, J. (1991) *Savage Inequalities*, New York, Crown Publishers.

Chapter 3

Foundational Qualities of an Ethical Person

Having outlined some of the moral problematics of schools, we may now discuss the deeper reasons why we find current practices in schooling ethically troubling. We find these practices troubling because we intuitively grasp that they run counter to the development of a truly ethical person. But what is our notion of a truly ethical person?

When we think about an ethical person we can think about that person in reference to specific actions performed by that person: she told the truth when concealing the truth might have been to her advantage; he canceled membership in a private club when, after discovering racial and sexual bias in its membership criteria, he was unable to get the board of directors to change the criteria. Beneath the specific actions performed at a specific moment in time, we can point to consistent or habitual tendencies to tell the truth, to respect each person for who they are, to be fair and objective. Beneath these tendencies toward specific virtues, we can recognize larger human qualities which form a foundation, so to speak, for these specific virtues and indeed for a whole life of ethical living. As one moves away from specific actions or choices towards these more basic, predispositional ethical qualities, one moves away from ethical disputes about what is the ethical thing to do in this specific instance, toward greater agreement that these general qualities are indeed foundational dispositions for ethical living. These qualities inform all ethical living, although, in any specific instance, the predominance of one quality over the others or the mix of all of them together will differ according to circumstances and perceptions. At this point in our discussion, I want to focus on these basic predispositions to ethical living, for they can provide a broadly acceptable and well focused foundation for our attempts at ethical education.

I believe that the truly ethical person acts as an autonomous agent, acts within the supports and constraints of relationships, and acts in ways that transcend immediate self-interest.[1] In other words, the ethical person has developed relatively mature qualities of *autonomy*, *connectedness* and *transcendence*. After exploring these foundational qualities of an ethical person, we may draw some general implications for a school which would educate such a person.

In speaking about these qualities, we must first recognize that children and youngsters develop these qualities over time. At any given time in their development, youngsters will exhibit greater or lesser strength in these qualities. Likewise, adults will vary in the strength of these dispositions, depending on whether their development toward maturity has been arrested or supported by significant people and circumstances of their lives. At present, we will explore these qualities as we might find them in a more fully developed adult.

It is also important to recognize that the sexes will express these qualities differently. Males are socialized, for better or worse, differently toward autonomy than females. The same is true about the qualities of connectedness and transcendence.[2] Although these foundational human qualities will be critical for the ethical development of both boys and girls, the mutual interpenetration of these qualities in the different sexes will be reflected differently at different stages and with different intensities in their development. As teachers move through the various stages of building an ethical school, the men and the women on the faculty will have to discuss these differences and their implications for the design of specific learning activities.

Autonomy

Ethical persons are autonomous. That is, they are independent agents who act out of an intuition of what is right or appropriate in a given situation. Their autonomy is in contrast to those who act out of a mindless routine, or simply because others tell them to act that way, or who act out of a feeling of obligation to or fear of those in authority. Autonomy implies a sense of personal choice, of taking personal responsibility for one's actions, of claiming ownership of one's actions.

Assumed in the notion of autonomy is the sense that the autonomous person is an individual. An individual is a person who has a sense of him or herself as standing out from the crowd. It does not mean necessarily an opposition to all that the crowd stands for. Rather it means a willingness to oppose the crowd in certain circumstances, to walk in a direction different from the crowd if it seems called for. It conveys a certain independence, a definition of one's self that is self-chosen, not imposed by anyone else.

Obviously one does not exist in isolation from communities of meaning and memory. To a great extent, one's identity as a person is formed as a male or female member of a specific cultural community, with its traditions, myths and mores. Yet one becomes an individual by appropriating the community's meanings and mores in a personal and unique way. At times one breaks through the standardized, routinized habits of thinking and acting into new ways of thinking and acting. If one is to overcome the suffocation of the collective, one has to choose one's own meanings. One has, in a sense, continuously to create oneself. Otherwise he or she becomes absorbed into the unreflective and undifferentiated ways of thinking and acting of the collective. This is the painful task facing young animals who are forced out of the nest to fend for themselves. For humans, it is the painful task of adolescence when one has to begin to separate from parents and from peers to forge one's own identity.

One forges one's own identity especially in creating a world of meaning. One's identity can be shaped by accepting the meanings which the culture conveys. There are customary ways to be feminine or masculine, to be successful, to be popular, to be good or to be bad. By simply doing what the culture (either the peer culture or the parental culture) dictates, one chooses an identity that is hardly differentiated from the generalized identities modeled by the culture. Others will seek to reject what the culture dictates in order to validate their individuality. Often that takes the form of radically different hair styles, clothing, language and counter-cultural music, dances and public heroes. The problem is that many others in one's peer group want to imitate the anti-establishment posture, and so one must go further and adopt an even more unique appearance within the antiestablishment group. Although viewed by adults as unhealthy or crazy, such behavior by adolescents is often a necessary interlude when youngsters can differentiate themselves. Unfortunately, because of involvement with drugs and alcohol, some attempts at self-definition often turn dangerously self-destructive.

However, the process of self-definition, begun in adolescence, goes on through young adulthood. After the first extreme efforts at differentiation, the process settles into a less flamboyant, but usually deeper journey. Assuming that one chooses not to conform to socially defined prescriptions, at least in certain defined areas of one's life, how does one justify these choices? Often such choices carry waves of anxiety with them, for they imply that one is cutting oneself off from society's definitions. Staying with what society prescribes offers security and approval. Striking out into the unknown puts our self at risk. To assume responsibility for one's life, to assert one's autonomy, to create one's meaning where none existed before, one needs to be strong to stand up to such anxiety. Fingarette captures this sense of anxiety very well:

> Responsibility is the readiness to face the absence of meaning, the nonbeing of self. It requires that a self *be* formed, a meaning be instated, a policy adopted. The crisis exists precisely because there is no a priori decisive resolution of the situation. Responsibility is the willingness to 'leap into nothingness'. But it is more than this: it is the willingness to accept . . . the consequences of one's act.[3]

From where does the strength to assume responsibility for one's life come? One source of strength comes from knowledge and understanding, although this knowledge is not necessarily scientific knowledge. Intuition and imagination also lead to knowledge and understanding. The strength comes from knowing that there are options, of knowing at least some of the options quite well. It also comes from knowing oneself well enough to know why one is afraid to define one's own meaning. (Those who live amidst grinding poverty and little hope, however, cannot see options and believe that they are already defined by outside forces.)

Becker, citing Adler and Fromm, asserts that 'neurosis is a problem of the authority over one's life'.[4] If one is afraid to move forward under one's own power, which is what it means to be autonomous, it is because that power has been turned over to someone or something else. In that case, one finds the source of power that sustains one's life externally to him or herself. The most common external source is the transference relationship in which one gets personal power from the father figure, from someone in authority. A second major source of power is from a supernatural, personal god, or some transcendent nature or world soul. A third source of power is in the cultural game itself, the everyday rituals and performances that are already in place and thoroughly scripted. Insofar as one turns over one's independence to any of these external sources of power, one loses autonomy.

The second source of power is sometimes the trickiest to negotiate. The history of religions is replete with stories and theological arguments about divine predestination and human freedom, about the preeminence of divine law simultaneous with divine emancipation from all burdens of the law. The answer, for some religious persons, seems to involve the paradox that God loves humans into a freedom that cannot be sustained unless it is shared with another, and with many others.

The strength to be free comes not simply from knowledge, even the therapeutic knowledge of our former bondage to an external source of power. The strength to be oneself can only be fully gained in relationships to other human beings. In authentic relationships, others give us the courage to be ourselves. Here we have the paradox of autonomy. One cannot be autonomous in isolation. Striving to be totally oneself by oneself reveals one's incompleteness, one's poverty, one's existential loneliness. One makes contact with 'reality', with the rich world of meaning, by reaching out beyond the isolated self. As Martin Buber put it:

> Human life touches on absoluteness in virtue of its dialogical character, for in spite of his uniqueness man [sic] can never find, when he plunges to the depth of his life, a being that is whole in itself and as such touches on the absolute. Man can become whole not in virtue of a relation to himself but only in virtue of a relation to another self. This other self may be just as limited and conditioned as he is; in being together the unlimited and the unconditioned is experienced.[5]

Our knowledge and our meanings and our uniqueness are validated in interpersonal relations. Our autonomy is both an independence and a choice to act in relation to others. Aggressive and adversarial competition then, is not natural; when it leads to selfish isolationism, it is in fact destructive of both the individual and the community. Buber offers a way out of the either/or conundrum of narrow individualism or constricting collectivism by showing that the depth of reality is essentially interpersonal. He offers us a vision of society working toward a transcending ideal, but an ideal rooted in autonomous individuals who find their fulfillment in living relationships.[6]

Dewey also speaks of society working toward this transcending ideal, an ideal in which human beings, working together, each with a reservoir of talent and intelligence, continuously recreate their society in progressive transformations, and in the process find their own individual fulfillment. He called this the ideal of democracy. In reality, Dewey acknowledged, democracy always falls short of the ideal, but continues to work toward that ideal. The human condition is defined both by the failure and the successes of that effort.[7]

The ethical person must be autonomous. Only in one's autonomy can one bring one's unique personal gifts to an ethical exchange. Only autonomous actors can claim responsibility for their choices. Only autonomous agents add a piece of their own lives, a quality of their unique selves to the ethical act. What constitutes the act as *ethical* is, as a matter of fact, that it is the intentional act of *this person*, not the act of an unreflecting, robot-like human who is following a routine prescribed by someone else, or is driven by irrational urges. Hence, we can see that one of the primary human tasks facing a young person is to become autonomous, to claim his or her own life. One can speak, then, of a deep moral obligation to become autonomous, for only then can one claim membership in a community of moral agents. It follows that the formation of autonomous persons is a primary ethical task of schooling.

Connectedness

The ethical person is connected. As we saw above, the autonomous person cannot authentically express her or his autonomy except in relationships. Every relationship is distinct. It offers unique possibilities because of the qualities which each person brings to the relationship. It is also bounded by the limitations which each person brings to the exchange. What one might expect from one person might be unfair to expect from another. A woman brings certain qualities to a relationship; a man brings other qualities. An older person might be expected to be more flexible in a relationship than a younger person; relationships involving people from the same culture are often different than those involving people from different cultures.

Circumstances set limits as well as create opportunities in relationships. Work related relationships hold opportunities for creative teamwork in technical areas; neighborhood relationships offer opportunities for more family oriented or recreational activities. Customer or client relationships are different than employer–employee relationships.

Hence it is clear that ethical behavior, while always involving interpersonal relationships, is shaped by the circumstances and status of the persons involved. Acting ethically requires one to be sensitive and responsive to the other person *within* the circumstances and the context.

Within this theme of connectedness, we cannot avoid discussing relationships between the sexes. Here it is so important to be sensitive to the revolution going on in the redefinition of what constitutes masculinity and femininity. Since this revolution is still in its beginning stages, it would be premature to attempt to redefine an education that 'correctly' socializes young people into the possibilities and responsibilities involved in male–female relationships. Yet some attempt must be made, starting from the recognition that traditional definitions of male and female are distorting of the possibilities for both males and females, in their separate lives and for their lives in relationships with one another. No longer can education about the human be dominated by male categories and male frameworks.

The school agenda for both males and females requires the simultaneous attention to equity and to difference.[8] Attention to equity requires that girls and boys have equal access to and encouragement in all programs in the schools. Attention to difference requires that girls and boys have opportunities for same-sex activities and for same-sex discussions of the social expectations of each sex role. It also requires appropriate cross-sex discussions of their differences and the issues and problems which flow from these differences.[9]

Attention to gender, circumstances and context, however, calls our attention to the cultural scaffolding of all relationships. One does not act with another person according to a uniform, universal script. Rather, humans express themselves in relationships according to an infinite number of cultural artifacts and cultural signs. The clothing one wears at various occasions, the language employed, the formality or informality one adopts — all these are culturally prescribed. Hence, acting ethically in any situation requires a knowledge of and respect for the culture one inhabits. Acting ethically means being sensitively connected to the values expressed by the sign and symbol system of that culture, for they make up the foreground and the background of relationships as they unfold. So it is not simply a question of one person in relation to another person; the relationship is supported as well as limited by the culture in which the two parties live their lives.

Every culture is a rich endowment, an enormous inheritance. It contains and expresses the history of a whole people over the course of many centuries: their struggles, their triumphs, their tragedies, their sense of heroism, their sense of failure, their ideals and their values. One acts ethically within that culture, within its possibilities and within its limits. No culture is perfect, no culture has finished its human journey. Hence the ethical person knows that the inheritance is also a burden. It has standards to be lived up to; it has standards to be surpassed; it has frontiers to be reached and perhaps expanded. Ethical persons, experiencing connectedness to their culture and to other persons, know that the culture sustains their lives, and that they have a responsibility to sustain the life of the culture. Sustaining that life happens in one's relationships and involves a kind of loyalty. Though the awareness is normally tacit, ethical persons approach one another as cultural beings, and yet because of the culture they share, they can approach each other in a discovery of uniqueness, where the humanity of the other person is discovered beyond, so to speak, cultural symbols, or as fresh embodiments of those symbols.

This adds, of course to the paradox of autonomy. One is autonomous, yet one's autonomy is as a cultural being.[10] As one supported by that cultural life, one bears responsibilities to it, to uphold its honor, its ideals, and to pass on the best of that culture to the next generation. The autonomous cultural agent, however, is different from the unreflective cultural agent who is a slave to the culture, who cannot distinguish the shortcomings of the culture — for example, in the way it treats women, or peoples of certain other cultures. The autonomous cultural agent can be a critic of his or her culture and see that as an act of responsibility to the culture. For beyond culture, there is humanity, to which all cultures bear responsibility.

Ethical beings are also connected to their natural environment. That environment provides air to breathe, food to nourish, the raw materials for food and housing, transportation and industrial production. This connection to nature in the present has a long past as well. Every person contains in his or her genes, so to speak, the history of evolution and the effects of cosmic time. As beings embedded in nature, yet having enormous power to affect nature, we have responsibilities to preserve the natural world itself, not simply to ensure the survival of the human species. Unbounded human exploitation of nature seemed a human right not very long ago. Now we recognize that we have to be far more respectful of natural processes of a nature that is endangered. Our connectedness to the earth is now seen as bringing ethical obligations to preserve the earth.[11] Our connectedness to the race, in both evolutionary time and in the future brings responsibilities both to our forebears and to our progeny.

We cannot leave this quality of connectedness without speaking of its political and social implications. In the United States, we happen to live in a democracy, which we are coming to realize is a fragile collage of many voices, many distinct communities. One view of democracy is that it is a society made up of separate individuals, each pursuing his or her own self-interest, joined together in a social contract which protects the rights of all individuals to pursue self-interest as long as it does not infringe on the rights of others. The problem with this view is that it ignores the real bonds that make life in the community morally compelling.[12]

Another view of democracy sees humans as inherently social, whose individual moral good is achieved and sustained only in community, through the bonds of blood to be sure, but also through the bonds of neighborliness, interdependence, and brotherly and sisterly affection. In this view, our humanity reaches its highest moral fulfillment in community. Without the relationships of community, which constitute not just necessary interdependencies, but also an intrinsic good, life would not be worth living. This is not to say that these relationships do not involve conflict, disloyalty, disagreement. But these relationships — even in conflict and struggle — define the context of human moral striving, the effort to agree on what constitutes our common good. Democratic political and social life does not guarantee a continuous experience of freedom, equality and brother/sisterhood; rather, those are the goals and purposes continually pursued in democratic give-and-take in public life. It is in being connected to that community with those very ideals, and the procedural rights and responsibilities that govern their pursuit, where we discover our truest moral selves.[13]

In discussing 'conscience as membership', Green makes a point of fundamental educational importance to the formation of a sense of connectedness.[14] He speaks of the necessity of empathy. In any discussion of what the group or social collective should do, there will be differences of opinion. In order for a moral choice to emerge (not simply an arithmetical calculation of allowing the consequences of X's opinion and Y's opinion to be figured into the decision, nor a calculation of political favor-swapping) one has to engage seriously the perspective of others. This means entering into an empathetic appreciation of the value and legitimacy of those perspectives, a kind of taking those perspectives as if they were one's own in order to understand the reasoning and to feel the affective colorations embedded within them. For our purposes, this insight into the psychological and existential dynamic of empathy enables us to see how one gains a sense of connectedness. It is by entertaining the legitimacy of the claims and perspectives of others, by imaginatively taking the reality of the other inside ourselves and seeing how it feels to be that other in these circumstances. This applies to the experience of being connected to family and ethnic roots, to friends, to the environment, and to the civic community. This dynamic of empathy provides the clue to developing the quality of connectedness in an educational setting, a dynamic that involves both understanding and feeling, a kind of sympathetic knowing.[15]

Transcendence

Transcendence is a term that might frighten some people off. For some it signifies an attempt to climb above our humanity, to leave it behind in a journey toward some higher, more spiritual form of life. This seems to be the Platonic ideal, where the philosopher ascends through a process of spiritual purification and mental abstraction to grasp the eternal form, The Good. I am not using the term in this sense. Rather, it has for me three levels of meaning, one dealing with the reach for excellence, the other with the turning of one's life toward something or someone else, and the third with achieving something heroic.

On the first level, transcendence means going beyond the ordinary, beyond what is considered average. In this sense, it means striving for and achieving a level of excellence that exceeds anything one has ever done before. The standard of excellence will be relative both to the type of activity involved (playing the violin, or high jumping, or writing poetry) as well as the person involved (a physically uncoordinated person, a mature professional athlete, a sight-challenged person). Transcendence on this level means a struggle to stretch the limits placed upon us by nature, to create a purer sound, to leap against gravity's pull, to see clear through to the essence of a feeling and capture it just so in the perfect metaphor. It is the struggle for the perfection of a human talent, and it is a struggle precisely because the possibilities of reaching that perfection, let alone of sustaining it, are limited by self-doubt and our very ordinariness as human beings.[16]

On another level, transcendence means going beyond self-absorption (which the search for excellence can sometimes promote) to engaging our lives with other people, whether to share their life journey with them, or to work with them towards some goal that benefits society in some way or other. Transcendence in this sense also means going beyond the ordinary. By the very ordinary nature of our social existence, we have to make room for others in our lives. People often intrude at times when we wish they wouldn't, but we respond to them with polite tact, and go back to our project as soon as their intrusion is over. We learn to accommodate others, sometimes cheerfully, sometimes reluctantly. This is what minimal or ordinary social relations requires. Transcending this level of social relations means taking on the burdens of others, caring for them, putting ourselves in their place — not once a month, but very often, if not habitually. It means anticipating their needs, surprising them with thoughtful gifts. It means finding our fulfillment in easing the burdens of others, making them laugh, helping them finish a project.

It also means being able to invest one's energies in a collective activity with others that serves some valued purpose beyond self-interest. That form of transcendence involves becoming a part of something larger than one's own life. Through that involvement one moves beyond an exclusive concern for one's own survival and necessities of life to an effort to serve a larger common good. That common good invests the actions of the individual with higher value, with higher moral quality.

As that involvement with others becomes more total, it moves toward the third level of transcendence, which is what I call the heroic. One can invest one's energies in other people and in a cause — up to a point. At some point, people say to themselves, 'OK that's enough for now. Now it's time for my life, my interests, my leisure and recreation.' The more total involvement is the willingness to sacrifice some of what most people would say were one's legitimate rights to 'time off', 'time for oneself'. Teachers who consistently stay late and arrive early in order to help out youngsters having difficulty with their school work, or just plain difficulty with life; social workers who consistently go the extra mile for their clients in getting them extra assistance; doctors who continue to spend quality time with their patients, listening to their anxieties; public officials who treat ordinary citizens with as much respect and courtesy as they do the 'important people'; store managers who spend countless hours devising ways to improve staff morale and customer service — these are people who are transcending the ordinary and embracing heroic ideals of making a difference in people's lives. The recognition of some of the great heroes, like Mother Theresa or Vaclav Havel, with public awards like the Noble Prize does not belittle the significance of the more everyday expressions of heroism.

Heroism, like transcendence, is often misunderstood. Heroes, it is thought, are those rare exceptions to the rule of self-interest, to the norm of mediocrity. While it is true that heroes are clearly outnumbered by the less than heroic, the *desire* for heroism is a common human trait. From our early childhood years onward, we ask, 'What is the value of my life?' We demand to be recognized, as Ernest Becker points out, 'as an object of primary value in the universe. Nothing less.'[17] Becker recognizes this as a desire to be, in one way or another, a heroic contributor to the human journey, and that nothing less will satisfy us.

Our interpretation of what constitutes heroic action is, of course, mediated by our culture and subcultures through the symbolic values it attaches to some achievements. A baseball batting average over .300, an Olympic gold medal, a scholarship to Oxford University, an Oscar-winning performance are all culturally significant, heroic activities. On a smaller stage, the neighborhood dominoes champion walks around his turf with heroic stride, for, in that ambiance, he is somebody to be reckoned with.

By claiming transcendence as a basic human quality we recognize that it is foundational to human moral striving. If this quality is not developed during youth and young adulthood, then a mature ethical life is simply not possible. Again, Green is helpful here in pointing to an educational source for nurturing this sense of transcendence, namely the great writers of imaginative literature.[18] In conversations with these poets of the heroic, these prophets and utopians, youngsters are exposed to the images of possibilities for human life. By exposure to stories of great human striving, their own heroic aspirations are kindled; these exemplars provide models for possible imitation. Biographies of great leaders in history bring reality perspectives to frame the more utopian idealism of imagination. The point Green makes is important, however: our transcendent aspirations are nurtured in and through the heroic imagination.

When transcendence is joined with the qualities of autonomy and connectedness, we begin to see how the three qualities complement and feed each other in the building of a rich and integral human life. Being autonomous only makes sense when one's autonomy can be in relation to other autonomous persons, when the uniqueness and wealth of each person can be mutually appreciated and celebrated. Connectedness means that one is connected to someone or something different from oneself. Hence it requires an empathetic embrace of what is different for the autonomous actor to make and sustain the connection. Community enables the autonomous individual to belong to something larger; it gives the individual roots in both the past and the present. However the community is not automatically self-sustaining, but is sustained by autonomous individuals who transcend self-interest in order to promote the common good, who join with other individuals to recreate the community by offering satisfying and mutually fulfilling services for one another, services of protection and support, care and help, joint action on a common project, celebration of a common heritage, honoring a community tradition by connecting one's own story to the larger story of the community. This give and take of life in the community simultaneously depends on and feeds the heroic imagination of individuals whose action, in turn, gives new life to the community.

Although we speak of these three foundational qualities of an ethical person in a somewhat abstract way, we don't want to think of them as a list of virtues which we set out to acquire. We are speaking of an ethical *person* who has a unity and integrity, whose actions reveal qualities that shine out as from a diamond. These qualities of an ethical person, however, do not fall from the sky. They are developed in action, through choices that are acted upon. These qualities are never achieved as an acquisition. They are always to be found in the action of specific persons in this moment, in these circumstances, with these people, and hence never perfectly or fully expressed. They are achieved only in the doing and in the doing-constantly-repeated.[19]

What I have described above is more like an ideal type of person. This person rarely if ever exists in perfect form. Most of the time human beings reflect imperfect efforts in the direction of truly autonomous, connected and transcending actions. The ideal type, however, serves a purpose. It points to an ideal we try to reach. It also provides a guide for those who would educate toward ethical living. By providing opportunities for youngsters to exercise autonomy, connectedness and transcendence, educators enable youngsters to experience the fulfillment and satisfaction of the way of being human. They learn the lesson that living ethically is the fulfillment of human nature.

If these qualities are foundational in a developing ethical person, then an ethical school will be concerned to nurture those qualities and discourage the development of their opposite qualities. Hence, teachers need to reflect on how they can use the everyday activities of youngsters in their classroom and other areas around the school to nurture these qualities. Of course, youngsters develop in recognizable patterns, so that what might be appropriate for a 10-year-old may not be appropriate for a 16-year-old. How one nurtures the sense of transcendence in kindergarten would differ from an approach taken in seventh grade. The three qualities can be supported in every grade, however, in ways that are suitable for the children, but it would be a mistake to expect all the children to manifest these qualities in the same way. Sex, race, culture and class will all nuance the child's expression of autonomy, connectedness and transcendence. Class-bound and ethnocentric teachers will have difficulty with such varied expressions. The sensitive teacher will observe the different expressions and listen to youngsters explain their behavior. Over time such teachers will be able to promote these qualities within an appropriate range of plurality and diversity.

Having presented a description of qualities basic to an ethical person, we now turn to the question of ethical systems of thought. That is, when we are faced with difficult or confusing decisions, how do we sort through them, make sense of them, find some principles by which to discuss options and the reasons behind the options and the meanings behind the consequences of each option. In the next chapter, we turn to ways of framing ethical questions so as to deal with them consistently and reasonably in an educating setting.

Notes

1 In the development of the ideas of this chapter, I have been helped by Ernest Becker's (1968) brilliant treatment of the ethical person in his *The Structure of Evil* (especially ch. 11) New York, The Free Press. His work is a synthesis of earlier works by Martin Buber, Max Scheler, John Dewey, Josiah Royce, Max Weber, Ralph Waldo Emerson and others. Emile Durkheim (1961), of course, has written the classic exposition on the centrality of autonomy and relationships to all moral actions in his book, *Moral Education* (trans. by E.K. Wilson & H. Schnurer), New York, the Free Press. I also found Thomas Green's treatment of moral education enormously appealing, but have chosen to focus on these three basic qualities rather than on his 'five voices of conscience', which I believe can easily be related to my trilogy. See Green, T.F. (1985) 'The formation of conscience in an age of technology', *The American Journal of Education*, **93**, pp. 1–38.

2 Carol Pearson speaks of six archetypes which both men and women adopt on their hero's journey through life. These archetypes provide a vocabulary for a wide range of human striving, and point to the developmental stages of the heroic journey most humans take. See Pearson, C. (1986) *The Hero Within Us: Six Archetypes We Live By*, San Francisco, Harper & Row.

3 Fingarette, H. (1963) *The Self in Transformation: Psychoanalysis, Philosophy and the Life of the Spirit*, New York, Basic Books, p. 101.

4 Becker (1968) p. 258.

5 Buber, M. (1955) *Between Man and Man*, Boston, Beacon Press, pp. 167–8.

6 Buber (1955) pp. 204–5.

7 Dewey, J. (1927) *The Public and Its Problems*, New York, Henry Holland Company, pp. 143–84.

8 Barbara Sichtermann (1986) treats this paradox very well in her book *Femininity: The Politics of the Personal* (trans. by John Whitlam) Mineapolis, University of Minnesota Press.

9 The literature on women's devlopment is considerable. A few significant books besides Sichtermann's follow: Gilligan, C. (1982) *In a Different Voice: Psychological Theory and Women's Development*, Cambridge, MA, Harvard University Press; Thorne, B., Kramerse, C. and Henley, N. (Eds) (1983)

Language, Gender and Society, Rowley, MA, Newbury House; Belenky, M.F., Clinchy, B.M., Goldberg, N.R. and Tarule, J.M. (1986) *Women's Ways of Knowing: The Development of Self, Voice, and Mind*, New York, Basic Books; Jordan, J. *et al.* (1991) *Women's Growth in Connection: Writings from the Stone Center*. New York, Guilford Press. For me, Virginia Woolf's *A Room of One's Own* (New York, Harcourt Brace, 1957), remains a pivotal book for raising awareness about women's oppression.

For books on male development see the following: Ong, W. (1981) *Fighting for Life: Contest, Sexuality and Life*, Ithaca, NY, Cornell University Press; Johnson, R. (1983) *He: Understanding Masculine Psychology*, San Francisco, Harper & Row; Raphael, R. (1988) *The Men from the Boys: Rites of Passage in Male America*, Lincoln, NE, University of Nebraska Press; Moore R. and Gillette, D. (1990) *King, Warrior, Magician, Lover: Rediscovering the Archetypes of the Mature Masculine*, San Francisco, Harper San Francisco.

For books in which the masculine and feminine are treated under the same cover, see Sanford, J.A. (1980) *The Invisible Partners: How the Male and Female in Each of Us Affects our Relationships*, New York: Paulist Press; Pearson, C. (1986) *The Hero Within Us: Six Archetypes We Live By*, San Francisco, Harper & Row.

10 See Shills, E. (1981) *Tradition*, Chicago, University of Chicago Press, and C.A. Bowers' (1987) development of Shills' ideas in his *Elements of a Post Liberal Theory of Education*, New York, Teachers College Press, on our embeddedness in our culture and traditions.

11 Gregory Bateson's (1972) challenging book, *Steps to an Ecology of Mind*, New York, Ballantine Books, seems to go too far in connecting our minds to a universal mind that is constantly at work in the universe, but his book has had a profound effect on many scholars who promote an ethic of ecological responsibility. Joanna Macy (1990) draws on his work in her essay, 'The ecological self: Postmodern ground for right action', in Griffin, D.R. (Ed.) *Sacred Interconnections: Post-Modern Spirituality, Political Economy and Art*, Albany, NY, State University of New York Press, pp. 35–48. For a remarkable account of an ancient people's sense of connectedness to the Earth and to their human history, see Bruce Chatwin's (1987) *The Songlines*, New York, Penguin Books; for a more philosophical perspective, see Max Scheler's (1957) classic, *The Nature of Sympathy*, London, Routledge & Kegan Paul.

12 See the excellent critique of both Locke and Hobbe's positions on the social contract in Robin Lovin's essay, 'Beyond the pursuit of happiness: Religion and public discourse in Liberalism's fourth century', in Palmer, P.J., Wheeler, B.G. and Fowler, J.W. (Eds) (1990) *Caring for the Commonweal: Education for Religious and Public Life*, Macon, GA, Mercer University Press, pp. 45–61.

13 Concerning this kind of political connectedness and the implications for education, see the following: Newman, F. and Rutter, R.A. (1975) *Education for Citizen Action: Challenge to the Secondary Curriculum*, Berkeley,

McCutchan; Janowitz, M. (1983) *The Reconstruction of Patriotism*, Chicago, University of Chicago Press; Butts, R.F. (1988) 'The moral imperative for American schools: . . . "Inflame the civic temper . . . " ', *American Journal of Education*, **96**, pp. 162–94.

14 Green (1985) pp. 13–14.

15 For a more elaborate account of the curriculum implications of sympathetic knowing, see Starratt, R.J. (1989) 'Knowing at the level of sympathy: A curriculum challenge', *Journal of Curriculum and Supervision*, **4**, 3, pp. 271–81.

16 See Martha Nussbaum's (1990) illuminating essay, 'Transcending humanity', in her book, *Love's Knowledge: Essays on Philosophy and Literature*, New York, Oxford University Press, pp. 365–91.

17 Becker, E. (1971) *The Birth and Death of Meaning*, 2nd Edn, New York, The Free Press, p. 76.

18 Green (1985) p. 24.

19 On this point, see Meilander, G.C. (1984) *The Theory and Practice of Virtue*, Notre Dame, IN, University of Notre Dame Press, p. 36–37.

Chapter 4

A Multidimensional Ethical Framework

In the previous chapter, we considered those basic human qualities that ground ethical choices in what is most natural and most fulfilling for human beings. We now move to more specific ethical systems by which the ethical content of situations may be illuminated. If we are seeking to build an ethical school we will need to develop an ethical framework which will give intelligibility to what is being designed. That is to say, we cannot start off in a scatter-shot fashion and suggest the first list of things to do that springs into our head. We need an overall framework that provides some unity and coherence to what we do.

In the field of ethics we can find a variety of frameworks which provide a rationale for a form of ethical education. Some would stress an ethic of justice as an overall framework; others would stress an ethic of care; still others would criticize those ethics as politically and culturally naive, preferring an ethic of critique. I want to suggest that we consider a large framework which embraces all three schools of thought in a multidimensional framework. That is to say, I believe that each of these schools of thought provides direction for an important part of an ethical education, but that no one of them taken alone is sufficient. When combined they complement each other in a richer response to the complex ethical challenges facing contemporary society.

What follows is not an attempt to develop a full blown ethical theory. That would be beyond the scope of this project. I am not so much concerned to build an ethical theory as I am to build an ethical school, to engage in the practice of ethics while engaging in the practice of education. Hence I will here discuss ethical themes and core ethical values, going somewhat into the arguments which support them, but without delving into the comprehensive philosophical blueprint which undergirds them.

Each theme will be developed consecutively. While attempting to remain faithful to the theory, or body of theory from which the theme was selected, the exposition will be guided by the ethical demands of the educating context. Underneath these three ethics, of course, are the irreducible assumptions and myths about what is valuable in human life in which every theory is grounded. A discussion of the ontology and epistemology behind these constructs, however, would paralyze, I fear, the very attempt to develop these thematic building blocks.

The Ethic of Critique

Since the historical moment appears to be one of transition and of transformation, as we move into a global market, a global information age, a global awareness of ecological catastrophe, it seems best to begin with the ethic of critique. Whether one begins from the less radical perspective of the recent proponents of school reform such as Boyer, Goodlad or Sizer,[1] or from the deeper critique of Apple, Bates, Freire or Giroux,[2] it has become increasingly evident that schools and school systems are structurally ineffective. Moreover, the awareness of the structural obstacles to renewal and change is taking on an historical dimension: the bureaucracy of school systems is coming to be seen as an enduring problem, not simply a contemporary phenomenon. Hence an ethic of schooling appropriately begins with the theme of critique, a critique aimed at its own bureaucratic context and the bureaucratic tendency to reproduce the status quo. As the school community under the leadership of parents, administrators and teachers, faces the possibility of creating an ethical school, it will also face the necessity to critique both the adversarial, contractual mindset of the unions, as well as the hierarchically structured impersonality of the governance and administration of the school. Beyond that critique awaits the critique of the overly (if not exclusively) technicist approach to teaching and learning tied to narrowly conceived learning outcomes and simplistic, quantifiable measures of learning.

Because it goes well beyond the functional critique of contemporary reformers such as Goodlad and Boyer, the ethic of critique developed here draws its force from 'critical theory', that body of thought deriving from the Frankfurt School of philosophers and others sympathetic to their perspectives.[3] These thinkers explore social life as intrinsically problematic because it exhibits the struggle between competing interests and wants among various groups and individuals in society. Whether considering social relationships, social customs, laws, social institutions grounded in structured power relationships, or language itself, these thinkers ask questions such as 'Who benefits by these arrangements?'; 'Which group dominates this social arrangement?'; 'Who defines the way things are structured here?'; 'Who defines what is valued and disvalued in this situation?' The point of this critical stance is to uncover which group has the advantage over the others, how things got to be the way they are, and to expose how situations are structured and language used so as to maintain the legitimacy of social arrangements. By uncovering inherent injustice or dehumanization embedded in the language and structures of society, critical analysts invite others to act to redress such injustice. Hence their basic stance is ethical for they are dealing with questions of social justice and human dignity, though usually not with particular, individual ethical choices.

Examples of issues confronted by critical ethics include sexist language and structured bias in the workplace and in legal structures; racial, sexual and class bias in educational arrangements, and in the very language used to define social life; the preservation of powerful groups' hegemony over the media, and over the political process; the rationalization and legitimation of institutions such as prisons, orphanages, armies, nuclear industries and the state itself. The point the critical ethician stresses is that no social arrangement is neutral. Every social arrangement, no matter how it presents itself as natural, necessary or simply 'the way things are', is artificial. It is usually structured to benefit some segments of society at the expense of others. The ethical challenge is to make these social arrangements more responsive to the human and social rights of all the citizens, to enable those affected by social arrangements to have a voice in evaluating the consequences and in altering them in the interests of the common good and of fuller participation and justice for individuals.

This ethical perspective provides a framework for enabling the school community to move from a kind of naiveté about 'the way things are' to an awareness that the social and political arena reflect arrangements of power and privilege, interest and influence, often legitimized by an assumed rationality and by law and custom. The theme of critique forces educators to confront the moral issues involved when schools disproportionately benefit some groups in society and fail others. Furthermore, as a bureaucratic organization, the school exhibits structural properties which may promote a misuse of power and authority among its members.

From a critical perspective, no organizational arrangements in schools 'have to be' that way; they are all open to rearrangement in the interest of greater fairness to their members. Where unjust arrangements reflect school board or state policy, they can be appealed and restructured. The structural issues involved in the management of education, such as the process of teacher evaluation, homogeneous tracking systems, the process of grading on a curve, the process of calculating class rank, the absence of important topics in textbooks, the lack of adequate due process for students, the labeling criteria for naming some children gifted and others handicapped, the daily interruptions of the instructional process by uniform time allotments for class periods — all these issues and others imply ethical burdens because they contain unjustifiable assumptions and they impose a disproportionate advantage to some at the expense of others.

The ethic of critique poses the fundamental ethical challenge to the school community: how to construct a school environment in which education can take place ethically? The ethic of critique reveals that the organization in its present form is a source of unethical consequences in the educational process.

Some would say that all organizations of their very nature tend in this direction. All organizations tend to make the rules and standard operating procedures the dominant force in organizational life, smothering initiative, instilling fear of not being promoted or approved by one's superiors, severely limiting freedom of choice, reinforcing 'group think' and the official rationalizations for the way things are. On the other hand, organizations, paradoxically, are the only places in the modern world where moral freedom and ethical creativity can be exercised in any significant way.[4] It is in the restructuring of human institutions to meet the human purposes for which they were originally designed that one finds significant moral fulfillment.[5]

Thus educational administrators will face the continuing paradox of their institutional position in the school. On the one hand, they must acknowledge the tendency built into management processes to inhibit freedom, creativity and autonomy, and to structure unequal power relationships, in order to ensure institutional uniformity, predictability and order. On the other, they must acknowledge their responsibility continually to promote that kind of freedom, creativity, and autonomy without which the school simply cannot fulfill its mission.

Hence the ethic of critique, based as it is on assumptions about the social nature of human beings and on the human purposes to be served by social organization, calls the the school community to embrace a sense of social responsibility, not simply to the individuals in the school or school system, not simply to the education profession, but to the society of whom and for whom the school is an agent. In other words, schools were established to serve a high moral purpose, to prepare the young to take their responsible place in and for the community.

Besides the legal and professional obligations, yet intertwined with them, the moral obligation of educators is to see that the school serves society the way it was intended. Hence, the challenge to restructure schools is a moral, as well as a technical and professional challenge.

The Ethic of Justice

One of the shortcomings of the ethic of critique is that it rarely offers a blueprint for reconstructing the social order it is criticizing. The problem for the school community is one of governance. How does the school community govern itself while carrying out educating activities? The ethic of critique illuminates unethical practices in governing and managing organizations and implies in its critique some ethical values such as equality, the common good, human and civil rights, democratic participation and the like. An ethic of justice provides a more explicit response to the question, even though that response may itself be flawed. We govern ourselves by observing justice. That is to say, we treat each other according to some standard of justice which is uniformly applied to all our relationships. The theory of justice we employ to ground those standards itself requires a grounding in an anthropology and epistemology. Plato explored this grounding in *The Republic*; his search was to be pursued by a long line of philosophers up to the present day.

Currently there are two general schools of thought concerning the ethic of justice. One school can trace its roots to Thomas Hobbes in the seventeenth century, and can find a contemporary expression in the work of John Rawls.[6] In this school, the primary human reality is the individual, independent of social relationships; the individual is conceived as logically prior to society. Individuals are driven by their passions and interests, especially by fear of harm and desire for comfort. Individuals enter into social relations to advance their own advantage. Individual will and preference are the only sources of value. Therefore social relationships are essentially artificial and governed by self-interest. The maintenance of social life requires a social contract in which individuals agree to surrender some of their freedom in return for the state's protection from the otherwise unbridled self-seeking of others. In this school of thought, human reason is the instrument by which the individual can analyze in a more or less scientific fashion what is to his or her advantage, and to calculate the obligations to social justice called for by the social contract. As Sullivan comments, in its more benign application, this theory conceives of social justice as 'a social engineering to harmonize needs and wants' of self-serving individuals in society.[7]

Lawrence Kohlberg carried on this tradition of moral theory, only he claimed to go beyond the traditional standoff between 'is' and 'ought' found in Hume and Kant.[8] Kohlberg claimed to have documented in his research an isomorphism between psychological development of moral reasoning and normative ethical theory.[9] His research indicated that as humans moved from one moral stage to a higher moral stage, they moved toward formal moral criteria of prescriptiveness and universality.[10] Their higher moral reasoning conformed to what moral theorists from Kant to Rawls had postulated as universal principles to guide ethical behavior. Once again, note that Kohlberg postulates the individual as the source of ethical judgment, and reason as the instrument of morality, although reason is now seen more in a developmental perspective.

The second school of thought on the ethic of justice finds its roots in Aristotle, Rousseau, Hegel, Marx and Dewey. They placed society as the prior reality within which individuality develops. Furthermore, it is through experience, through living in society that one learns the lessons of morality. Participation in the life of the community teaches individuals how to think about their own behavior in terms of the larger common good of the community. In this school freedom 'is ultimately the ability to realize a responsible selfhood, which is necessarily a cooperative project'.[11] Ethics is grounded in practice within the community. Hence the protection of human dignity depends upon the moral quality of social relationships and this is finally a public and political concern. Citizenship is a shared initiative and responsibility among persons committed to mutual care.

From this perspective, a communal understanding of the requirements of justice flows both from tradition and from the present effort of the community to manage its affairs in the midst of competing claims of the common good and individual rights. That understanding is never complete; it will always be limited by the inadequacy of tradition to respond to changing circumstances and by the impossibility of settling conflicting claims conclusively and completely. But the choices will always be made with sensitivity to the bonds that tie individuals to their communities.

Kohlberg himself believed that moral reasoning and choices were best made in a communitarian setting.[12] He played an active role in the formation of 'just community' schools. Hence, it can be argued that an ethic of justice, especially when focused on issues of governance in a school setting, can encompass *in practice* the two understandings of justice, namely, justice understood as individual choice to act justly, and justice understood as the community's choice to direct or govern its actions justly. In a school setting, both are required. In practice, individual choices are made with some awareness of what the community's choices are (school policies), and school community choices are made with some awareness of the kinds of individual choices that are being made every day in the school.

A school community encouraging an ethic of justice will see to it that specific ethical learning activities are structured within curricular and extra-curricular programs. This may mean extensive faculty and student workshops on active listening, group dynamics, conflict resolution, values clarification, problem naming, etc. Teachers familiar with Kohlberg's stages of moral reasoning could more easily understand the general frame of reference students are using, for example, instrumental hedonism, negotiation of the social contract, etc.[13]

In a school that takes site-based management seriously, issues of the day-to-day governance of life in the school are inescapable. The ethic of justice demands that the claims of the institution serve both the common good and the rights of the individuals in the school. Ongoing discussions of student discipline policies, of faculty and student due-process procedures, of agreements about faculty time commitments, etc., are absolutely necessary. Furthermore, classroom discussions of issues within the curriculum will need to be carried on for the moral questions they raise about personal as well as public life in the community. Approaches to multicultural education should include not only the standard attempts to create better understanding of cultural differences, but also discussions of historical and present social conditions which breed unjust relationships between people of different cultures and explorations of ways to alter those social conditions. Issues of grading and testing could be examined from the perspective of justice, with such discussions leading to the development of alternatives to present practices which benefit some to the disadvantage of others.

No doubt such freewheeling discussion of so many taken-for-granted elements of schooling will get messy and unmanageable. Most educators dread such initial lack of definition. On the other hand, the debate is in itself educative. The only way to promote ethical attitudes and understandings about self-governance is to engage in it.

Even this brief treatment of the school's involvement in promoting an ethic of justice points to the close relationship of the ethic of critique and the ethic of justice. In order to promote a just social order in the school, the school community must carry out an ongoing critique of those structural features of the school that work against human beings. Often the naming of the problem (critique) will suggest new directions or alternatives for restructuring the practice or process in a fairer manner. For example, a school policy that provides a disproportionate share of resources to students with grades in the upper decile of the student body results in inequities that impact unfairly large numbers of 'average' students.[14] It raises questions about the responsibility of brighter students to share their gifts for the larger good of the community, perhaps in some peer tutoring activities.

The Ethic of Care

One of the limitations of an ethic of justice is the inability of the theory to determine claims in conflict.[15] What is just for one person might not be considered just by another person. Hence discussions of what is just in any given situation can tend to become mired down in minimalist considerations. (What minimal conditions must be met in order to fulfill the claims of justice?) In order for an ethic of justice to serve its more generous purpose, it must be complemented or fulfilled in an ethic of love. While earlier discussions of the incompleteness of the ethic of justice took place in a theological context,[16] more recent discussions have tended to ground the ethic of love and caring in a philosophy of the person.[17] Scholars such as Gilligan and Noddings have promoted these ethical directions from a vantage point of psychology, especially women's moral development, in the current literature on the ethic of caring.[18]

Such an ethic focuses on the demands of relationships, not from a contractual or legalistic standpoint, but from a standpoint of absolute regard. This ethic places the human persons-in-relationship as occupying a position for each other of absolute value; neither one can be used as a means to an end; each enjoys an intrinsic dignity and worth, and, given the chance, will reveal genuinely loveable qualities. An ethics of caring requires fidelity to persons, a willingness to acknowledge their right to be who they are, an openness to encountering them in their authentic individuality, a loyalty to the relationship. Such an ethic does not demand relationships of intimacy; rather, it postulates a level of caring that honors the dignity of each person and desires to see that person enjoy a fully human life. Furthermore, it recognizes that it is in the relationship that the specifically human is grounded; isolated individuals functioning only for themselves are but half persons; one becomes whole when one is in relationship with another, and with many others.

A school community committed to an ethic of caring will be

grounded in the belief that the integrity of human relationships should be held sacred, and that the school as an organization should hold the good of human beings within it as sacred. This ethic reaches beyond concerns with efficiency, which can easily lead to using human beings as merely the means to some larger purpose of productivity, such as an increase in the district's average scores on standardized tests, or the lowering of per-pupil costs.

A school committed to an ethic of caring will attend to the 'underside' of the diverse interactions among members of the community, that is, to those motives that sometimes intrude, even slightly, on an exchange with a teacher, student or parent.[19] Sometimes those motives involve the desire to dominate, to intimidate, to control. Sometimes those motives involve racial, sexual, ethnic and age stereotypes that block the possibility of honest communication. Sometimes a teacher feels insecure in the face of strong and assertive students and feels the need to put them in their place. Sometimes an administrator is not even aware of the power she or he has in the eyes of teachers and recklessly toys with the teacher's insecurity by some lighthearted ridicule of a classroom activity.

When these underside issues dominate an exchange, they block any possibility of open and trusting communication. Mistrust, manipulation, aggressive and controlling actions or language on the part of an administrator, teacher or student can lead to relationships that are hypocritical, dishonest, disloyal and dehumanizing. An exchange between a teacher and student can move beyond a superficial ritual to a contractual obligation to a relationship of caring, when there is a deep attention to the unique human beings involved in the exchange, to issues of self-esteem, personal confidence and ego anxieties. People who are fairly secure in their sense of themselves and in their professional role are not overly affected by these underside motives; few, however, are entirely free from them in every circumstance. If these motives are understood and acknowledged initially, they will not distort the exchange in excessively manipulative or negative ways.

Besides developing sensitivity to the dignity and uniqueness of each person in the school, educators can promote an ethic of caring by attending to the cultural tone of the school. Often the use of language in official communiqués will tell the story: formal abstract language is the language of bureaucracy, of distance; humor, familiar imagery and metaphor, personalized messages are the language of caring. Through reward procedures and ceremonies as well as school emblems, school mottos, school songs and other symbols, the school communicates what it cares about. When the school rewards academic competition in ways that pit students against each other, when the awards are few and go only to the top students in the formal academic disciplines, then the school makes a clear statement of what it values. Other ceremonies and awards that stress caring, cooperation, service, teamwork, etc., send different messages. Some schools clearly promote a feeling of family and celebrate friendship, loyalty and service. Laughter in the halls, frequent greetings of each other by name, symbols of congratulations for successful projects, frequent displays of student work, hallways containing pictures of groups of youngsters engaged in school activities, cartoons poking fun at teachers and administrators — these are all signs of a school environment that values people for who they are. When youngsters engage every day in such a school community, they learn the lessons of caring, of respect, of service to each other. With some help from peers and teachers, they also learn how to forgive, to mend a bruised relationship, to accept criticism, to debate different points of view.

The ethics of caring brings us full circle at this point. Knowing our own failures to care for others, our own immature ways of rationalizing moral choices, knowing our own reluctance to challenge questionable school arrangements, we are able to confront the general weakness in the human community. That weakness is part of being human. Despite our heroic ideals, we often act in distinctly unheroic ways. Hence a sense of compassion is needed for one who would act ethically, compassion for him or herself, and compassion for others. We have to extend our caring to forgiving. The forgiveness extended, we then go on with the business of making things right. And then forgive again.

Two Questions

There remain two questions, the response to which may close out this inquiry into a multidimensional ethical framework for educators. The first question involves the legitimacy of combining themes derived from three different ethical theories, despite what some might claim are irreconcilable differences among the theories.[20] The second question deals with the practicality of the construct for educators. Namely, does it offer them a perspective which allows them to frame or name the most important ethical issues encountered in schools and to shape an environment that encourages ethical choice?

I believe that the three theories are not irreconcilable. They can be grounded on both the essential nature of human beings and on the essential nature of human society. That is to say, one can argue for the necessary interpenetration of each theme by the others if one is to argue for a fully developed moral person and a fully developed human society. Even a superficial familiarity with the themes suggests that each theme implies something of the other theme: the ethic of critique assumes a point of view about social justice and human rights and about the way communities ought to govern themselves; the ethic of justice assumes an ability to perceive injustice in the social order as well as some minimal level of caring about relationships in that social order; the ethic of caring does not ignore the demands of community governance issues, but claims that caring is the ideal fulfillment of all social relationships, even though most relationships among members of a community function according to a more remote form of caring.

Moreover, each ethic needs the very strong convictions embedded in the other: the ethic of justice needs the profound commitment to the dignity of the individual person; the ethic of caring needs the larger attention to social order and fairness if it is to avoid an entirely idiosyncratic involvement in social policy; the ethic of critique requires an ethic of caring if it is to avoid the cynical and depressing ravings of the habitual malcontent; the ethic of justice requires the profound social analysis of the ethic of critique in order to move beyond the naive fine-tuning of social arrangements in a social system with inequities built into the very structures by which justice is supposed to be measured. The response to the first question, then, is that the themes are not incompatible, but, on the contrary, complement and enrich each other in a more complete ethic.

The response to the second question is likewise affirmative. An educator's day is filled with ethical situations and challenges. Sometimes those situations clearly call for a critique of an unfair school procedure; sometimes they call for a sensitive guiding of student discussions of ethical issues embedded in the material under study; sometimes they involve debate over school policy in an effort to balance the common good with individual rights; sometimes they involve the demands of an individual person to be recognized and cherished for who she or he is. At other times, more complex problems require that the school board examine the problem from each framework, and perhaps balance the demands of all three ethics in its response to the problem. Given our proactive position, namely the building of an ethical school, the larger framework of all three ethical themes offers a more comprehensive and multidimensional foundation for such a construction. Figures 4.1 and 4.2 offer a visual diagram of how the themes work together to provide such a multidimensional perspective.

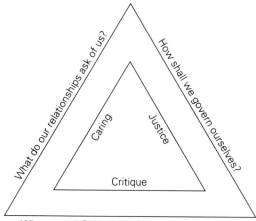

Figure 4.1: The multidimensional ethic

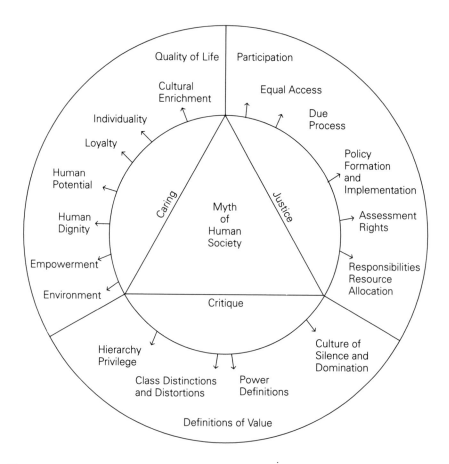

Figure 4.2: The multidimensional ethic at work in a school setting

This chapter has attempted to develop a tapestry of ethical perspectives woven of three themes: the theme of caring, the theme of justice, and the theme of criticism. An ethical consciousness that is not interpenetrated by each theme can be captured either by sentimentality, by rationalistic simplification, or by social naiveté. The blending of each theme encourages a rich human response to the many uncertain ethical situations the school community face every day, both in the learning tasks as well as in its attempt to govern itself.

Notes

1   Boyer, E. (1983) *High School: A Report on Secondary Education in America.* New York, Harper & Row; Goodlad, J.I. (1984) *A Place Called School,* New York, McGraw-Hill; Sizer, T.R. (1984) *Horace's Compromise: The Dilemma of the American High School,* Boston, Houghton Mifflin.
2   Freire, P. (1970) *Pedagogy of the Oppressed,* New York, Herder and Herder; Apple, M. (1982) *Education and Power,* Boston, Routledge and Kegan Paul; Bates, R.J. (1987) 'Corporate culture, schooling, and educational administration', *Educational Administration Quarterly,* **23**, 4, pp. 19–115; Giroux, H.A. (1988) *Schooling and the Struggle for Public Life,* Minneapolis, University of Minnesota Press.
3   See, for example, Adorno, T.W. (1973) *Negative Dialectics,* New York, Seabury; Habermas, J. (1973) *Legitimation Crisis,* Boston, Beacon; Horkheimer, M. (1974) *Eclipse of Reason,* New York, Seabury; Young, R. (1990) *A Critical Theory of Education,* New York, Teachers College Press. This literature is complemented by feminist as well as minority cultural critiques of society and schooling.
4   Max Weber, often mistakenly identified as a proponent of bureaucracy, saw both its dangers and its possibilities for moral initiation. An illuminating exposition can be found in the introduction of S.N. Eisenstadt's (1968) book, *Max Weber: On Charisma and Institution Building,* Chicago, University of Chicago Press.
5   Starratt, R.J. (1990) *The Drama of Schooling/The Schooling of Drama,* London, Falmer.
6   Rawls, J.A. (1971) *A Theory of Justice,* Cambridge, MA, Harvard University Press.
7   Sullivan, W.M. (1986) *Reconstructing Public Philosophy,* Berkeley, CA, University of California Press.
8   Kohlberg, L. (1971) 'From is to ought: How to commit the naturalistic fallacy and get away with it in the study of moral development', in Mischel, T. (1971) (Ed.) *Cognitive Development and Epistemology,* New York, Academic Press, pp. 151–235.
9   Schindler, D.L. (1986) 'On the foundation of moral judgment', in McLean,

G.F., Ellrod, F.E., Schindler, D.L. and Mann, J.L. (Eds) *Act and Agent: Philosophical Foundations for Moral Education and Character Development.* Lanham, MD, University Press of America, pp. 271–305.

10   Kohlberg (1971) pp. 224–5.

11   Sullivan (1986) p. 22.

12   Blatt, N. (1970) 'Studies on the effects of classroom discussion upon children's moral development', unpublished doctoral dissertation, University of Chicago': Kohlberg, L. (1980) 'High school democracy and educating for a just society', in Mosher, R.L. (Ed.) *Moral Education: A First Generation of Research and Development.* New York, Praeger, pp. 20–57; Higgins, A., Power, C. and Kohlberg, L. (1984) 'The relationship of moral atmosphere to judgments of responsibility', in Kurtines, W. and Gerwirtz, J. (Eds) *Morality, Moral Behavior, and Development,* New York, Wiley Interscience.

13   Kohlberg, L. (1981) *The Meaning and Measurement of Moral Development,* Worcester, MA, Clark University Press.

14   See the study by Cusic, P.A. and Wheeler, C.W. (1988) 'Educational morality and organizational reform', *American Journal of Education,* **96,** pp. 231–55.

15   Hollenbach, D. (1979) *Claims in Conflict,* New York, Paulist.

16   Neibuhr, R. (1935) *An Interpretation of Christian Ethics.* New York, Harper & Brothers.

17   MacMurray, J. (1961) *Persons in Relation,* London, Faber; Buber, M. (1970) *I and Thou,* New York, Scribner.

18   Gilligan, C. (1977) *In a Different Voice: Women's Conception of Self and Morality,* Cambridge, MA, Harvard University Press; Noddings, N. (1984) *Caring: A Feminine Approach to Ethics and Moral Education,* Berkeley, CA, University of California Press.

19   Starratt, R.J. (1984) 'The underside of supervision', *Impact,* **19,** pp. 5–16

20   Pateman, C. (1980) 'The disorders of women: Women, love and the sense of justice', *Ethics,* **91,** 1, pp. 20–34.

Chapter 5

What Might an Ethical School Look Like?

The core ethical perspectives of justice, care and critique provide what Richard Peters calls the *form* for ethical considerations.[1] They contain ethical principles that help make choices reasonable. They guide conduct, but they do not supply the *content* of moral choices. We always find ourselves in specific circumstances which provide the content of our choices; the ethical frameworks help us to see what principles are involved in the choices which that set of circumstances presents us. Hence, guided by the ethic of caring, I may choose to settle a grievance indirectly through the mediation of a mutual friend. The ethic of caring does not determine that I have to settle the grievance this way. It simply makes that a reasonable and sensible choice in those circumstances. Similarly, I may choose to say no to the one more drink 'for the road'. The ethic of justice (observance of the law) or the ethic of care for myself and others make this a sensible choice. What I want to do now is supply some of the content to our ethical school. Guided by these ethical frameworks, what are essential elements which would constitute an ethical school?

What follows is an attempt at a comprehensive picture of an ethical school. The imaginary description assumes that such a school did not fall out of the sky; long and sometimes painful deliberations would have gone into the building of such a school. We will consider the journey required to get to this comprehensive ethical school in subsequent chapters. For now we are trying to answer the question, 'What would a truly ethical school look like?' Our general response is that it is a school that fosters ethical practice as well as understanding. It is based on the premise that if one wants to learn ethics, one must practice ethics.

This picture of an ethical school is comprehensive; that is, we are looking at the school in a full expression of its ethical quality. Piecemeal attempts to nurture ethical development in youngsters are praiseworthy, but they will not be nearly as effective as a thorough and consistent school-wide effort. When youngsters encounter various teachers throughout the school day who model ethical values, when ethical concerns are discussed in various subjects across the curriculum, when multiple opportunities are present to practice the ethic of caring, the ethic of justice and the ethic of critique, when guidance counselors, coaches and moderators of student activities all consistently speak about ethical concerns, when the school corridors are hung with posters which reflect ethical values of self-respect, loyalty and honesty, and when the school and the home express consistent concern over ethical issues, the message is pretty hard to ignore.

Such a comprehensive and consistent teaching of ethical concern may be the final stage of a long process of school renewal. It may have taken several years to approach this comprehensive effort. For now, we want to see what might constitute the end product of such a comprehensive effort.

A truly ethical school will nurture the ethical growth of all members of the school community through an interlocking pattern of three levels of the organization of the school: the level of curriculum, the level of extra-curricular activities, and the level of institutional support. That is to say, the staff of the school has to build into the academic program, the extra-curricular program, and the various mechanisms of institutional support an abundance of opportunities for youngsters to learn, through practice, what it means to be an ethical person and to be a member of an ethical community.

What follows is not an absolute prescription of what every school should look like. Rather, it is intended to serve as an illustration of what one school might look like. Stimulated by this description of a truly ethical school, others can come up with more appropriate alternatives and organizational patterns to suit their circumstances.

Institutional Support

Philosophy Statement

The school would have a philosophy statement which describes its institutional sense of identity. Within that statement we should be able to find statements like the following:

The school is committed to promoting a sense of community as well as an individual sense of self-worth.

Our school is to be a community of caring and fairness, a community of life-long learners for whom knowledge is both a cherished inheritance and a critical achievement.

The school community governs itself democratically, cherishing freedom, responsibility and integrity within an ongoing search for a communal sense of purposes and values. Every member of the school is vital to and responsible for the quality of life of the school.

In such philosophy statements there would be an espousal of core values such as responsibility, honesty, tolerance, loyalty, courtesy, compassion, integrity, fairness, care and respect. The philosophy statement would then be echoed throughout other institutional support mechanisms, such as the parent–student handbook, the school senate bylaws, the home–school association bylaws.

The School Senate

Ethical concerns are necessarily social. Ethics is intrinsically bound up in a community's efforts to govern itself. Hence, the school would have some institutional mechanism of self-governance, such as a school senate. This would be the primary vehicle of internal governance of the school community. Within the general policies established by the school board, this body would establish the specific policies and guidelines by which the school members conduct their business. This body, or a subunit of it such as the school court, would serve as the last appeal within the school for matters that cannot be resolved by members through ordinary procedures established for managing the day-to-day affairs of the school. Only in disputes involving civil law, after the school senate has failed to settle the matter, would appeal be made to the school board. The school senate would carry on its business through its own subcommittee structure (for example, a curriculum committee, a budget committee, a discipline appeals committee, a school court, a home–school committee, etc.) and would meet in full session once a month to consider matters which these subcommittees judge to require the full deliberation of the senate. The senate shall be made up of four parents, eight students, twelve teachers and two administrative staffpersons, or some arrangement reflecting those proportions. The senate subcommittees may include additional non-voting members drawn from the school community as it appears appropriate.

Within the policies set down by the school board, the superintendent, the principal and other administrators will continue to administer many of the traditional, day-to-day details of the operation of the school, such as the drafting and administering of school-wide budgets, oversight of safety and scheduling arrangements, coordinating the meetings and activities of various staff and parent committees, and so forth. The senate will convey to the school administrators the conclusions of its deliberations which will require administrative follow-through. Administrators will bring to the senate for its deliberation major policy issues which require resolution. Where they cannot be resolved within the senate, they will be referred to the school board.

Student Government

There will also be a student government. The eight student members of the school senate will be drawn from the student government. Membership on the student government is seen as an honor. Students in academic or disciplinary difficulties may lose their membership, or be ineligible for membership.

The student government will coordinate a Big Brother/Big Sister program whereby upper classpersons take responsibility for helping younger students in a variety of ways (peer tutoring, listening to their problems and anxieties, taking them to school events and interscholastic games, etc.). Being chosen as a Big Brother or Big Sister will be considered a privilege. Students in academic or disciplinary difficulties will forfeit that privilege.

The student government will also coordinate the efforts of the student conflict-resolution teams. These teams, who go through a special training every year, are made up of students who help other students work out their problems in non-violent and non-destructive ways. Students experiencing disciplinary difficulties may be referred to these teams by the school administration. Students may seek help from these teams voluntarily as well. The teams will serve an ombudsman role, from time to time, when students feel they are unable to resolve a misunderstanding or negotiate a relationship with a teacher or administrator.

The student government will coordinate awards and student recognition events with a committee of the school staff. Various leadership awards, school spirit and service awards, and awards named in honor of local or national leaders will be a special part of each year's graduation ceremonies.

The student government will coordinate the various student committees responsible for working on revisions of the student handbook. Such revisions will be considered every other year. Recommendations for revisions will be passed along to the appropriate school senate committee.

The student government will name the members of the principal's student advisory committee. This committee will work with the principal on student concerns and how the administration might attend to them. Similarly, the principal will seek their advice before acting on complaints about serious student misbehavior which carry major sanctions.

The student government will coordinate the various social events of the school year such as dances, picnics, school Olympics, the school fair, etc. They will also assist at parent–teacher evenings by running the coat room, preparing refreshments, managing the baby sitting room, etc.

The Home–School Association

The home–school association will be the umbrella organization for communications and activities involving parents. Where possible, a room with necessary amenities such as telephone, coffee pot, computer terminal and printer, filing cabinets and desks, and a conference table will be available for parents who are working or meeting in the school. The home–school association will provide parent volunteers for a variety of tasks. These tasks include the following: helping youngsters with remediation exercises, working as teacher aides, assisting in enrichment activities, helping in the library, helping supervise the cafeteria, hallways and playgrounds, acting as traffic control aides at the start and end of the school day. When appropriate, parent-and-student teams will help with school repairs or school cleanup days. Members of the home–school association will serve on welcome teams to visit new families who have moved into the attendance area. They will also work with the school administration and guidance department in certain cases where families may need other adults to help them with a family problem. The officers of the home–school association will meet with the school administration regularly to discuss parental concerns. Their monthly newsletter to all the parents will be one of the primary means of the school communicating with parents about school-wide activities and noteworthy events.

The home–school association will also sponsor several social events during the year. These might include pot-luck dinners for parents (providing teachers and administrators an opportunity for informal conversations with parents); a major meeting at the beginning of the school year when the school staff may review the values which the school is attempting to promote; a musical comedy put on by the parents for the students and faculty in which the foibles of parents and family life are portrayed and provide everyone with a good laugh; a school picnic in the spring when the school staff and the students prepare the food for the parents, and various awards are presented to parents.

The Guidance System

Teachers, school guidance personnel, the school psychologist and social worker will pursue five goals with the students:

1　to build community;
2　to develop positive interpersonal skills;
3　to develop versatility in problem solving and decision making;
4　to promote habits of good health;
5　to develop self-esteem.

Using a variety of settings and processes, from individual counselling, to group discussions, workshops, etc., the staff will seek to promote healthy personal and social growth. They will work with the student government on the training of the conflict-resolution teams. They will also develop crisis intervention plans for a variety of student crises. Some of this work will involve members of the home–school association in working with family situations. They will be responsible for coordinating special programs for students with severe and chronic discipline problems. The guidance department or school psychologist and social worker will also conduct at least one faculty workshop a year to facilitate teachers' work with students in the home base program (see description below).

Scheduling

The school will provide a schedule which provides time for a variety of valuable learning opportunities. Besides a flexible schedule for regular academics, the school schedule will allow time for weekly group guidance sessions run by the guidance department and the teachers, the daily home base session, assemblies in which members of the civic community address the students about issues in the community, and the enrichment afternoon program.

For high schools and middle schools, the home base program is a fifteen minute daily session that has replaced the homeroom.[2] In order to keep the student home base groups to a relatively small number, every member of the school professional staff including librarians, counselors and administrators are assigned a home base group. Daily announcements and attendance are covered, and then the group has some time to report on issues that need taking care of, topics that need to be discussed, home base projects kept up to date, etc. It is a time for the adults to listen as well as to counsel. Attention to problems in studies, problems at home, interpersonal problems at school — this is a time to identify them and to schedule follow-up. Every home base moderator, who stays with the same group for two years, is responsible for monitoring the academic and social development of the youngsters in that home base. Communications with parents are expected on a regular basis and teachers and administrators who are having difficulty with students are expected to talk to the students' home base monitors.

Every student is expected to participate in the enrichment program. This is a special time period after academic classes when students can participate in extra-curricular activities. The extra-curricular clubs also make up the intramural teams in a variety of sports. One afternoon a week, each extra-curricular club plays in intramural games. In schools with varsity athletics, the teams practice after the enrichment period.

The school will sponsor a school fair each year. Various clubs will sponsor booths and special activities such as skits, choral singing, jazz ensembles and various games. There will be prizes given to the faculty for the most creative costumes and for the most comical skit representing an unusual classroom scene. A prize will be awarded to the best desert prepared by the home–school association. Multicultural booths will exhibit artifacts, food and music indigenous to the various cultures. The school fair is an annual celebration of the diverse talents within the school community.

Symbolic Expressions of the School Identity

The school will have a school song, a school motto and a school emblem or mascot. All of these shall express the central values which define the school's identity. On appropriate occasions of solemnity and celebration, students and staff will sing the school song. The school motto will be displayed conspicuously around the school building. It should be printed on the school stationery and on school diplomas. A school pin with the motto inscribed will be given out as a prize for various student achievements. Reference to the school motto and to the school song in a variety of circumstances help to remind all members of the community that they belong to a school that stands for these values. If the school bears the name of a famous person, then the values of that person should be expressed in the school song and the school motto. If a school does not have a school song or motto, a competition among students and teachers to compose a song or a motto will be held, with the whole school, including the home–school association, voting for the final selection.

The Discipline Program

The school has a consistent and explicit discipline program which is based on five basic principles which the school attempts to support throughout the daily activities of school life. The five principles are:

— Treat others as you would be treated.
— Take pride in your work.
— Take responsibility for yourself.
— Be generous, for you have received much.
— Be a friend.

While it has been necessary to draw up specific rules consistent with these principles, these rules have been kept to a minimum.

Within classrooms and various student activities, however, there are to be found explicit rules which govern the type of activities which are allowed. Each classroom teacher, for example, is expected to draw up a contract with the students for what kind of behavior is to be expected. Students will have a say in determining those rules, but once agreed to, they will be expected to adhere to them. Each student is to bring home copies of those classroom contracts, and the parents are expected to sign the contract and return it. Their signature indicates their willingness to support the agreements reached in the classroom contract. Where parents have questions about the classroom contract, they should discuss them with the teacher.[3] Once a month teachers and students will discuss how the contract is working, and how it might be improved.

If a student feels that he or she has been unfairly treated in a disciplinary case, the student may appeal to the discipline appeals committee. This committee, made up of students and teachers, will hold a hearing, calling witnesses if necessary. In cases of minor infractions involving minor penalties, the decision of the appeals committee will be considered final. If the situation warrants it, the appeals committee may request parental consultation, assistance from the guidance department or from a conflict resolution team. In cases where major harm has been done to an individual or to the school, and where the penalties involved are serious and long-term, the appeals committee may, if it cannot resolve the matter, refer it to the school court.

The school court, made up of parents, teachers and students, will hear cases involving serious and long-term penalties. Whenever a student is to appear before the school court, the student's parents will be notified. The court may refuse to hear a case, leaving the decision made by a school official to stand. Students and their parents may appeal a decision of the school court to the school board, which may or may not decide to hear the case.

In cases involving repeated complaints about student misbehavior in group settings, the principal will seek advice from the student advisory committee of the student government. Whenever possible, the student government will be expected to influence group behavior of students in constructive directions.

The Student–Parent Handbook

The school provides every family with a student–parent handbook. This handbook is put together every year with the joint efforts of the student government committee on the handbook, the school senate subcommittee on the handbook, and the home–school association subcommittee on the handbook. The handbook contains the statement of the school philosophy and the calendar of the school year with the major events noted. The handbook also includes the academic policies on homework, parental access to student records, student assessment procedures and requirements for promotion. A section on discipline follows, including the statement of the five principles, school-wide regulations, classroom contracts and procedures to be followed when parental involvement is solicited by the school. The handbook also contains information about extra-curricular activities, field trips, parent participation in the home–school association, and on the use of the school by parent groups. The first general meeting of the parents provides an opportunity for reviewing the contents of the handbook. The school considers the handbook a kind of general agreement between the parents, students and staff about how the community will conduct its business during the year.

There may be other institutional supports for this ethical school. In general, the institutional supports attempt to make the school 'user friendly', to exhibit an ethical quality, a welcoming, human face.

Ethics and the Academic Program

Throughout the academic program, teachers will create opportunities for class discussions of ethical issues and for projects that carry ethical import. Such discussions and projects will serve to nurture the basic qualities of autonomy, connectedness and transcendence in developmentally appropriate ways. There may be occasions within these discussions and projects to bring one or more of the ethical frameworks of justice, critique and care into play. Over time, students would develop facility with the language and point of view of each of these frameworks.

In lower grades, these discussions can involve story-telling about their local heroes, for example, or about a time when someone did something really nice for them. Teachers would tell stories about people who exemplified specific virtues which the children might emulate. Teachers might design simple games which the children could play at home with a parent or sibling, games in which they learned to follow rules, or games that rewarded truth telling or being generous to others.

Children would be encouraged to create their own birthday cards for members of their families and for their friends. They could also create cards for other occasions such as Valentine's Day, Father's and Mother's Day, etc. Once they have learned the great satisfaction that these greetings bring to others, they might be encouraged to 'adopt' a grandparent in a nursing home, or an elderly neighbor who is confined to his or her house or apartment, and make cards with special greetings and news from school for them.

Once a week, teachers might take fifteen minutes for children to respond to the question, 'What have I done this week to make someone happy?' By listening to the stories of other children, members of the class will pick up ideas to try out in their own lives.

There will be concerted efforts to generate respect for the talents of each person. Teachers will have the children write out all the things they can do well. After that has been shared among the class, they would write out all the things they do not do well or cannot do at all (for example, cannot swim, or cannot play the violin, or cannot fix a car). The teacher can point out that some children may never be able to excel at some of these activities or talents, but that everyone will have some talent at which they can excel. These discussions can turn gradually toward the notion of disability, how some children are born with certain physical challenges which make it difficult or impossible for them to do certain things. Just as they themselves have some things they find difficult or impossible to do, these other children have other disabilities. On the other hand, these children also have things they can do exceptionally well, sometimes because of their disability. Thus a sight impaired person develops very sensitive hearing and touch, and a hearing impaired person develops visual acuity which surpasses the normal visual sensitivity of others. These kinds of discussions will help youngsters with various kinds of disabilities feel more at home among their peers, and deflect the kind of stereotyping children sometimes fall into when the term 'disability' is used. Children will be encouraged to talk about their feelings toward another child who can do something much better than themselves. They will be encouraged to reflect on those things which they can do better than most other children, and realize that everyone has something to offer, and that everyone should be respected for who they are, rather than be disrespected because they cannot do certain things.

These suggestion barely scratch the surface of the abundance of possibilities for teaching ethical qualities to young children. Books such as Thomas Lickona's *Educating for Character*, and Lamme, Krogh and Yachmetz's *Literature-Based Moral Education* present a treasure chest of good ideas and excellent sources.[4] Appendix I contains the names and locations of various groups which are developing ideas and materials for use in the elementary grades.

In middle school and high school youngsters are developing a sharper sense of themselves and a clearer awareness of the complexities of relationships. They are learning to stand apart from others, both peers and adults, in order to establish their own individuality and autonomy. It is during these years that youngsters have to struggle with the seemingly conflicting demands of being part of a group or a family and being an individual. While they need some group identity as adolescents, as separated from adult society, they also need to try out possible bridges to that adult world which they know they must eventually enter.

As they lurch from assertive independence to group conformity to exploratory excursions into adult relationships, these youngsters need to experience an adult environment of caring, security and authentic conversation. While the school will want to expose them to ethical challenges of the adult world, there will be more than enough lessons to be learned about ethical living in their own experience. This experience contains many of the perennial ethical questions: How can I be myself, when everyone else wants me to conform to their norms? How can I communicate with someone I really like, when I don't know if they are at all interested in me? How do I make up after a fight? What talents do I have that I can offer the world? How do I assert my own opinion without making someone else's opinion look foolish? Why should I obey the rules, when I see others flaunting them? How can I be liked by others when the cost of belonging seems to require that I do things I consider wrong or stupid? What if people really knew how stupid and confused I feel? How can I overcome my fear of failure and ridicule and just be myself, instead of hiding behind all the disguises of conformity? How can I make a difference in such a large and complex world? What is there that deserves my life-long best effort? How do I balance having fun with getting my work done?

While adults have more or less come to terms with these questions, they have a painful immediacy for adolescents. When the agenda of the school seems to have no relevance to those questions, when adults seem totally unaware of or indifferent to the world-shaking significance of these questions, then adolescents create their own world, separated from the adult one.

Without turning the classroom into the therapist's couch, the teachers in our ethical school will explore the connections of the curriculum to the journey which these young people are making. Once those connections are made, the students will more readily apply themselves to the work. As their work in school grows more connected to their lives, the school can begin to expand their awareness that their lives are connected to a larger world, a world that needs them. They will begin to understand that the issues they are struggling with are found in that larger world, and that their ability to come to terms with these issues, as they find them in their lives now, will better enable them to participate in the struggles of that larger world.

Some specific examples may illuminate the above generalizations. In narratives and poems, teachers can find many examples of human beings struggling with the same questions adolescents face. Teachers can lead students to making these connections by having them ask questions such as, with reference to Mark Twain's *Huckleberry Finn*, 'Is Huck Finn like me?' 'How is he like me, and how unlike me?' Those questions will reveal a variety of responses. The teacher can go on to ask the question, 'How would you feel if you were Jim (the runaway slave)?' which would open up a series of other responses. Note that in the course of these discussions, the teacher is pursuing an intelligent analysis of the novel, as the syllabus prescribes. The teacher, however, will be simultaneously engaging youngsters in the ethical implications of the characters' lives as well. Depending on the circumstances, the discussion can evolve into a fuller discussion of slavery, or race relations, or Mark Twain's own attitudes as revealed in the novel, etc. In this case, the discussion should spill over into the students' own experiences of race relations.

In some instances the literature teachers will coordinate their classes with the social studies teachers. Along with their study of *Huckleberry Finn*, students might encounter other historical accounts of slavery in the United States before the American Civil War. After studying the stratagems employed in the Underground Railroad by which some slaves were enabled to escape to the north, students might stage a mock trial of a white person who was caught helping slaves to escape. The prosecution could argue that the prisoner was violating the law (which he or she would have been) and therefore deserved to be punished. The defense could argue for the higher principle involved. The jury would have to debate the ethics of their own decision.

The teachers in both classes might continue to probe the experience of African Americans both during the period of legalized slavery and after the Civil War, when their plight became worse in some cases. Discussions of present day realities of race relations, when conducted with sensitivity, can help students of various racial backgrounds confront the human costs of racial injustice for all members of society.[5] Especially if the school is a multicultural school, these discussions will need to continue beyond the classroom in a variety of settings such as student government meetings, home base sessions, the principal's advisory council, home–school association meetings, etc. Clearly the ethical issues involved here encompass both the personal realm as well as the sociopolitical realm. It is in the lived experience of the students, however, that the practice of ethical behavior *vis-à-vis* race relations will be worked out. How honestly and thoroughly they confront how they get along among themselves will affect how they get along in the larger world of adult society.

In science classes there will be ample and appropriate opportunities to discuss public policy issues related to the material the class is treating. For example, in biology classes, teachers may raise ethical concerns over genetic engineering and medicinal drug experimentation standards. In chemistry classes, the students might explore the toxicity of various chemicals and how they affect the water table as well as the upper atmosphere. Acid rain and its effects on the environment; the costs of anti-pollution controls and of alternative technologies; chemicals put into food products and their effects on the body — these and other issues raise questions of public policy and legislation about which every citizen should be informed. In the study of physics, issues such as the generation and disposal of nuclear wastes; the varieties and costs of energy conservation; the physics of outer space defense technology; the danger of electro-magnetic radiation effects on the human body provide fertile ground for probing ethical implications in personal and sociopolitical life.

In social studies, fundamental questions about how humans govern themselves should run throughout the curriculum. That question relates directly to how the school community governs itself. Specific issues of participation, freedom of speech and assembly, property rights, and so forth, are to be found in the students' experiences in the school. How the school negotiates the various stresses and strains between individuals pursuing their own agendas and the maintenance of order in the common pursuit of the school's purposes provide many concrete examples of what the civic polity faces in its daily effort to govern itself. As students make connections between their own experiences of governing themselves individually and collectively and the experience of the civic community's experience of governing itself, they should begin to study some of the larger mechanisms involved in this effort at self-governance. These mechanisms include the various agencies at the local, state and federal levels charged with various tasks such as maintaining roads, sewers, energy sources, transportation systems, communications systems, health systems, educational systems, police and judicial systems, interstate commerce systems, banking systems, welfare systems, tax systems, etc. The regulation of these agencies is under the direction of lawmakers, in the state legislature and town councils. All of these are guided by a sense of what policies serve the common good of the community, state and nation. These public policies inevitably involve ethical choices. Hence it is imperative for students, as young people close to the age of voting, to make themselves knowledgeable about various alternatives in public policy, for that is how, through their political activity, they can influence the common good of the community.

In the upper grades, students need to be drawn towards the larger concerns of global government, for that is the overriding reality of the world in which they will live. Questions of caring, justice and critique can be raised about the realities of global trade, global food distribution, global environmental protection, transnational corporations, international religious bodies, economic communities such as the newly formed European Economic Community, international banking, the World Court, the United Nations, etc. Obviously, these larger issues will be more appropriately treated in the upper years, due to their complexity.

The effort in social studies should not be to make students extensively knowledgeable about every issue. Rather, it should be to enable them to know how to make themselves knowledgeable, where to find appropriate information, what kind of questions to ask of politicians, which advocacy groups are available to pursue certain issues in greater depth and with greater political influence.

In the humanities, students should be brought to encounter human tragedy and heroic achievement, virtuous as well as despicable examples of human behavior. In the process of encountering both heroic and villainous characters in literature, they should be asked to reflect on questions of human purpose and fulfillment.[6] Their exposure to literature and art must necessarily reflect the multicultural world of the present and of the future. They must come to appreciate the great literature and art of many cultures so as to take pride in their own culture and honor the achievements of other cultures. As they encounter various characters in various settings, they may be encouraged to put together a personal philosophy about life, what they esteem, what they pity, what their own heroic ideals are, how they want to live their lives as adults. Such attempts to clarify what for them are profound human meanings will fill out the more conceptual scaffolding of their ethical principles.

This treatment of the possibilities within the academic curriculum for ethical learning is altogether too brief. It is meant simply to be suggestive. Experienced teachers would be able to generate many more examples of specific ethical lessons they could teach within the material that makes up their present curriculum.

Ethics and the Enrichment Program

The enrichment program applies more to the middle and high school levels than the elementary, although some modified version of it might be tried there. It involves all those activities normally called extracurricular activities. I suggest the name enrichment because its purpose is an enrichment of the learning agenda being developed in the academic program. Besides the other learnings involved in the enrichment program, the program is intended to support the development of the three foundational qualities of autonomy, connectedness and transcendence, and to teach the ethical frameworks of justice, critique and care.

The enrichment program will run for about ninety minutes every day after the academic classes. The intramural program is considered part of the enrichment program and will involve the various clubs on one of the five days. In the upper grades, varsity athletes will be expected to coach various intramural teams. Clubs and activities will meet three or four times a week during this period. Occasionally a school assembly or some other activity such as a student debate on a controversial issue in the community or a school concert will take up the enrichment period.

Everyone will be expected to participate in the enrichment program. There will be enough clubs and groups to accommodate a wide variety of interests among the whole student body. All of the clubs and groups will have a service orientation. That is, each club or group is expected to make some kind of a contribution to the school community or to the larger civic community. Where possible and appropriate, all the professional staff will serve as moderators to the clubs or groups. In some instances, a parent or qualified adult volunteer from the community may serve as moderator. At the end of each semester, students must choose a different enrichment activity. Upper classpersons, interested in pursuing something in greater depth, may repeat an earlier enrichment activity. Membership in clubs will be decided by a committee of the faculty, after students have indicated their first three choices. In cases where students' first three choices are not available, the student and the home base moderator will work out an alternative choice. The clubs will be made up of students from at least three grade levels.

The types of clubs available could include the following: model United Nations, the ecology club, the Student Government, the drama club, the art club, the pottery club, the photography club, the school newspaper, the poster club, the debate club, the candlemaking club, the needlepoint club, the science club, the Spanish (German, Irish, French, Polish, Arabic, Russian, African, Japanese . . .) club, the calligraphy club, the bonsai club, the math club, the chess club, the community service club, the junior chamber of commerce club, the architecture club, the garden club, the kite club, the fabric design club, the choir, the jazz ensemble, the oral history club, and so forth. While the community service club would be involved in a variety of volunteer services in the civic community, all clubs could participate in some form of community service. For example, the ecology club might volunteer to clean up a park, or the Spanish club might volunteer to act as translators for newly arrived Hispanic immigrants. Many of the clubs would prepare displays and activities for the school fair. The community service club would be responsible for the annual school-wide food and clothing drive for the needy.

The school would display many of the products from the clubs in the many display cases around the school, with such displays changing every week or so. In every club, older members of the club are expected to help teach younger members the various skills and approaches used in their activities. When appropriate, members of the civic community will be asked to judge the productions of various clubs, such as the pottery and the kite clubs, the photography and the needlepoint clubs. While these outside judges help to provide some recognition of excellence, there will be no grade assigned for participation in the enrichment program, although the activities will be noted on the students' transcripts.

Moderators will be expected to attend to various ethical learnings that easily emerge out of the nature of the activities involved in the enrichment program. In some cases, it will involve the lesson of recognizing the integrity of the work at hand (Green's conscience of craft);[7] in other cases, the lesson of teamwork (Green's conscience of membership);[8] in other cases, an appreciation of another cultural perspective (Green's conscience of imagination).[9] Throughout the activities of the enrichment program, moderators will encourage a sense of pride in one's work, a generous sharing of one's talents with others, a willingness to talk through alternative solutions to difficult problems, a concern to make a contribution to the life of others, and an appreciation of the talents of others.

Variations

Building on the illustrative model above, it would be possible to build variations of this model into an ethical school which might be more responsive to specific communities of parents and students.

The African American School

Suppose that the community being served by the school was almost 100 percent African American. In the middle school and high school years, much more attention might be given to themes important to the African American community. Every effort would be made to enlist the participation of parents in the life of the school. Where that has happened, there is clear evidence of greater student involvement in their studies.[10]

Certainly the literature of the African American people themselves would be given greater attention. That literature is enormously rich and culturally fertile, even though it is unknown to the majority of white educators. Their poetry expresses the complex struggle to define themselves apart from the definition of white people.[11] Their stories tell of suffering and loss, of a natural love for life, an anger masked in humor, and an indomitable hope, sometimes mixed with bitter resignation.

Young African Americans need to own their heritage and to come to terms with how that heritage defines their present search for heroic possibilities. It would be senseless to attempt to encourage an ethical commitment to a sociopolitical life, to a world of work, to a personal integrity among African Americans without encouraging this appropriation of their cultural heritage. Furthermore, any realistic education has to deal in depth with how they will negotiate their future in a society defined by white culture and white economic and political power. That future may take many shapes, but those who attempt to prepare them for that future need to see it in its pain as well as its possibilities.

More than anything, young African Americans need to develop their many human talents, their strengths, and a sense of themselves that will carry them through the struggles that lie ahead of them. In one sense, they are the ones who will redefine the United States of America, they and the other 'minorities' who are on the threshold of constituting the majority. What that redefinition will be remains to be seen, but there is no doubt that their years in school will, for better or worse, affect that redefinition.

The Multicultural School

In most urban schools, multiculturalism is the reality. The mix of cultures is made up of a variety of communities, such as African American, Mexican American, Hispanic Central American, Cambodian, Eastern European, Portuguese, Chinese, Philippino, Caribbean, Japanese, Vietnamese, etc. In such settings, the ethical development of these young people would attempt two things at once. On the one hand the school will attempt to develop pride in one's cultural heritage, and on the other, to develop a sense of community across cultures.

In this effort, the home–school association will be critical. A thorough orientation of the teachers to the cultures of the children should be of the first order. The home–school association can sponsor a variety of seminars and workshops to develop sensitivity to the various differences among the cultural communities represented in the school. Where possible, parents from each cultural community would be enlisted as teachers' aides, so that the students can see adult models from their own communities. The home–school association can sponsor many social events which encourage a mixing of parents. How students hear their parents speaking about other cultures will influence how they react to others in school.

The curriculum, while observing the requirements in the mainstream academic disciplines, will have to accommodate bilingual and bicultural students. While science and mathematics courses may require a certain uniformity, the humanities and arts classes provide a more flexible framework for including literature and art from the various cultures.

In the student government, the school would insist on representation by students from various cultural groups. In a sense, the workings of the student government represent a kind of miniature United Nations. These students must be brought to the realization that their ability to govern themselves and to develop a sense of community during their school years will affect the way they forge their adult lives in a nation made up of many cultures.

The enrichment program will provide a healthy way to mix youngsters from various cultures into cohesive groups working together on group projects. In the course of working together, they can learn much about the wealth of the cultural heritage each person brings to the task.

The Big Brother/Big Sister relationships can be used both to support links between students of the same culture as well as to forge links between students of divergent cultures. Similarly, home base groups can help the mixing process. The school fair will provide another opportunity for various cultural groups to represent their cultural heritage. Perhaps as a sign of their unique contributions as a culture to the consolidation of the community, a tree planting ceremony might be held each year, with each cultural group being responsible for the choice of the tree that had a special significance in their culture, on a rotating basis from year to year. The tree could symbolize something given by a cultural group to benefit the whole community. Furthermore, the school could celebrate the many national and international days, such as United Nations Day, Earth Day, Human Rights Day, World Food Day, as opportunities to underscore their unity within diversity.

Magnet Programs

Especially in the eleventh and twelfth grades, schools could provide interdisciplinary programs which provided options to students to develop leadership talents in specific areas. For example, a high school might have a two year sequence for eleventh and twelfth grade students that combined social studies and science, focusing on public policy and the environment. This course would consider the legal, economic, ecological and quality of life issues surrounding many public policy debates such as global policy efforts on oceanic exploitation, atmospheric pollution, alternative energy resources, disease control, sharing of technology, chemical and biological arms control, nuclear waste disposal, etc. Students in this program would be expected to develop public policy positions and to interact with state and federal agencies regarding these policies.

Another magnet program might involve a two year intensive program dealing with a variety of public service professions and the public issues and problems with which they are dealing. In such a program, students would be expected to spend some time out in the field working and gathering information about a specific government agency, such as the urban planning commission, the district attorney's office, the housing commissioner's office, the local environmental protection agency, the department of youth and family services, the police department, the highway department, the consumer protection agency, the tax collection agency, etc. They would be expected to research problems and issues which local citizens have had with such agencies, and to get the perspectives of the people working in the agencies. They would be expected to put together proposals for the improvement of services and of information access to the public, and to suggest improved ways for citizens to communicate with these agencies.

A third magnet program could involve an extensive treatment of geopolitical issues. Students would study the various economic and political blocs around the world, such as the European Economic Community, the oil producing countries, the Southeast Asian Alliance, and so forth. They would also study the workings of the United Nations, the World Bank, the World Court and other international agencies dealing with global issues. The point of this magnet program would be to interest the students in careers and leadership opportunities involved with global matters. As they studied the various unresolved global problems, they would be expected to critique various proposals that have been offered, and to come up with proposals of their own. Correspondence with various international agencies, including the United Nations, and perhaps a visit to some of them, would provide first-hand contact with the people engaged in such careers.

The possible variations on the original illustrative model of the comprehensive ethical school are numerous. These ideas were mentioned simply to point out how various contexts might elicit various designs.

Summary

The point was made earlier that one learns to be ethical by practicing ethical behavior. Reviewing a comprehensive picture of an ethical school should enable us to see how a school may, in providing youngsters many opportunities to behave ethically, develop the habit of being ethical. The opportunities to behave ethically are reinforced by the chance to discuss ethical issues in the classroom, in home base, in enrichment activities, in student government, and in a variety of other home and school settings. When the school and the home reinforce ethical learning through layer upon layer of activities, then the lessons learned have a much better chance of taking permanent root.

It may be obvious that building such an ethical school is a major undertaking. It will require a great deal of restructuring of the school. What is presented here are examples of how it might be done within a relatively traditional framework of schooling. There may be other ways to restructure the school to make its ethical teaching even more effective. Having reviewed these examples, we might be ready to ask how building such schools might be possible for an ordinary community. We will address that in the next chapter.

Notes

1 Peters, R. (1973) *Authority Responsibility and Education*, 3rd Edn, London, George Allen & Unwin.
2 I have stolen this idea from one of my students, Richard Weisenthal, who created a similar arrangement in his middle school.

3 See the detailed system of discipline worked out by Richard L. Curwin and Allen N. Mendler (1988) in *Discipline With Dignity*, Alexandria, VA, Association for Supervision and Curriculum Development.

4 Likona, T. (1991) *Educating for Character*, New York, Bantam Books; Lamme, L.L., Krogh, S.L. and Yachmetz, K.A. (1992) *Literature-Based Moral Education*, Phoenix, Oryx Press.

5 For an insightful discussion of this topic, see Steele, S. (1991) *The Content of Our Character*, New York, Harper Perennial.

6 Edna O'Brien has put it well: 'When Chekhov, that most dissecting of writers, decides to devote 183 pages in "The Duel" to the history of a discontented man whose wife is dying, whose children are neglected, and whose sexual urges cannot be met, it is not simply a little tale of infidelity; it is the gouging of the human heart, the moral prig as well as the moral dodger in us all, the insatiability of human nature and the little graph of each private fall.' And again, 'Books are the Grail for what is deepest, more mysterious and least expressible within ourselves. They are our soul's skeleton.' O'Brien, E. (1993) 'It's a bad time out there for emotion', *New York Times Book Review*, February 14, p. 20.

7 Green, T.F. (1985) 'The formation of conscience in an age of technology', *American Journal of Education*, **93**, pp. 4–7.

8 Green (1985) pp. 7–15.

9 Green (1985) pp. 22–24.

10 See Comer, J. (1988) 'Educating poor minority students', *Scientific American*, **259**, 5, November, pp. 42–48.

11 See, among others, the commentary on African American explorations of the racial self in literature by Gates, H.L., Jr. (1987) *Figures in Black*, New York, Oxford University Press.

Chapter 6

Building an Ethical School: Launching the Project

This chapter marks a shift away from the more theoretical considerations which serve as a foundation for building an ethical school to the more practical concerns of actually attempting to put such a project in motion. The next few chapters attempt to outline a plan of action. Such a plan of action should not be taken as the single universal blueprint. Local histories, local politics and local group dynamics will dictate their own special blend of planning strategies. What these chapters contain are illustrations of basic planning principles. It is important to consider the principles as primary and the illustrations as secondary. Moreover, the plan assumes a school that accepts the theoretical propositions outlined in earlier chapters. In many instances, schools will add to or modify these foundational building blocks. With these points in mind, let us move ahead to the business of launching the project.

Prerequisites

Before launching into a major effort of building an ethical school, the leaders of the school should check to see whether several prerequisites to such an effort are reasonably in place. The first prerequisite is that they have a reasonably solid *idea of what they want to do*. This assumes that they have taken the time to discuss foundational ideas about ethical education such as are found in the preceding chapters and their references. They might have spent some time delineating the moral problematics of the school as they see them. They should have arrived at some sense of what operational descriptors would define minimum and maximum levels of success for the project. (The previous idealized description of what an ethical school might look like would provide an example, perhaps, of a maximum level of success.) They should also have taken stock of the potential willingness of the parents to participate extensively in the project and how much work it will involve developing and nurturing parental leadership. They should then consider the time frame for the project, namely, how many months and years they estimate for each phase of the project, and what will be the resources needed for each phase of the project. The point of elaborating on this prerequisite is that the school leaders should have a sense that they know what they are talking about, and that others will have the same impression. It does not mean that they should have everything completely and thoroughly worked out; as a matter of fact, they should be only at that point where they realize how much they need the rest of the school community to fill out their initial, preliminary vision.

The second prerequisite is *trust*. This project is going to require most of the adults involved with the school (teachers, administrators, parents, support staff, central office staff, school board members) to engage in a collaborative effort. Such collaboration is difficult when various groups among these adults do not trust one another.

To be sure, in any organization or group there will be some antagonisms, some jealousies, some misunderstandings, some insecurity, and some unreasonable use of power and authority. Perfection eludes us all. On the other hand, despite these realities, many groups and organizations can work together in relatively effective ways when there is a sufficient level of trust that, despite the personal agendas at work, everyone is working toward the agreed upon goal in agreed upon ways with a reasonable amount of moral integrity. Where such trust is lacking we find various individuals withholding effort, witholding information, sequestering resources, making private agreements and deals, protecting turf and status — all of which spells disaster or at least a slow death to any large collective effort. If the leaders feel that sufficient levels of trust do not exist within the school community, then the first task of building an ethical school becomes the effort to build trust among the members of the school community. That in itself may take up to two or three years. Without it, however, the project will not succeed. With it, the project has a good chance of succeeding. The literature on human relations in organizations and on school community relations should provide some guidance here.

The third prerequisite is a prevailing sense of *confidence*, especially among the teachers, but also among parents and administrators, that the school community can solve its problems, that it can create something special in that school. This prerequisite assumes a healthy sense of empowerment, namely, that people have the skills and imagination individually and collectively to create a lively and effective educational environment which really promotes the growth of youngsters. It assumes a sense of efficacy in teachers, both individually and collectively, that they can devise learning activities and strategies that can promote learning in even the most recalcitrant or disinterested students.[1] Again, if the leaders of the school perceive that teachers in the school are not accustomed to taking curriculum matters into their own hands, if they are not used to working in teams to solve instructional or management problems, then they should be given some experiences doing just that.

This may point to more of an administrative problem than a teacher problem. Administrators sometimes control the decision-making structures in a school so tightly that teachers have to come to them constantly for permission to deviate from the syllabus or to solve a problem they are having with a student. Administrators need to communicate an assumption that teachers as professionals know how to deal with the day-to-day variables that occur in classrooms and corridors. They need to encourage teachers to exercise the discretion necessary for any professional to deal with individual circumstances which neither school policies nor textbooks nor curriculum plans cover with sufficient specificity (nor could they ever). If teachers individually and collectively experience this kind of professional autonomy and efficacy, then they will be ready to participate in the ambitious effort of building an ethical school.

A word of caution on the prerequisites. In one sense, a school community will never be entirely ready to launch this project. School leaders can be caught in the stranglehold of analysis paralysis, never being certain that there is *enough* trust, and *enough* confidence in the faculty. If on a rating scale of one to ten the leaders can rate their school community above a five on these prerequisites, then they should be able to feel reasonably confident that the project has a good chance of succeeding. If the rating is down around a two or a three, then they should hold off and work on strengthening the prerequisites.

The First Step

The leaders of the school should do an initial, but quiet survey of what good things the school is currently doing in what might loosely be called ethical education. They might attempt to organize their findings under some of the categories developed in earlier chapters, for example, dividing their findings under curricular programs, enrichment programs and institutional supports, sorting the student learnings according to learnings being promoted under the categories of autonomy, connectedness and transcendence, and then sorting the student learnings again according to the ethic of justice, the ethic of care and the ethic of critique. They might make a list of specific values they find being promoted (honesty, respect, conformity, individuality, competition, obedience, achievement, friendliness, loyalty, generosity, etc.) and those they find being opposed (cheating, violence, creativity, scapegoating, sexism, curiosity, lying, excluding others, etc.).

This initial survey will provide them with plenty of illustrative material in the next several months when they discuss the project with others. It will also enable them to speak about all the good things that are currently going on in the school, thus avoiding giving the impression to the staff that the project is a punishment for their not doing their job. They should also be attentive to areas where, with just a little effort, new advances can be made toward concrete ways of building an ethical school. This will enable them to create opportunities for some initial successful efforts, thus building an increased sense of efficacy for teachers and parents. They may also want to note some of the values that are currently being promoted which are questionable, and some values that are suppressed which should not be.

The Second Step

The leaders of the school now need to pull together an *ad hoc* team of teachers. This should be done with no fanfare. The team should be made up of sufficiently diverse people who enjoy diverse spheres of influence among their peers. The school leaders should present the project in general terms, indicating that this will eventually become a school-wide effort to build something that is doable and something of which everyone involved can be proud. They can point to some of the things the school is already doing in this regard. They will want to emphasize that what they have in mind is something that should not require additional teachers, nor necessarily a longer school day or school year. What is being sought is a qualitative enrichment of what they are currently doing so that, besides being academically effective, they can likewise improve the moral impact of the school on the youngsters.

Assuming that this initial team of teachers agrees to work on the project, they should be encouraged to read some foundational literature on ethical education such as the material found or referred to in the previous chapters. There should be time set aside, perhaps one afternoon every two weeks, for the team to meet to discuss the readings and to explore implications for their school. They might, perhaps, be asked to draw up their own statement of the moral problematics of their school as a first step towards achieving some focus, as well as exploring the diversity of points of view on the team. The development of process skills of discussion, arguing a point of view without attempting to force another to agree, listening carefully to other perspectives, finding points of commonality and agreement, being able to summarize points of agreement and disagreement, being able to build and arrive at consensus — all these will help them to develop the leadership skills for leading other groups as the process unfolds.

The Third Step

The school leaders should go to the superintendent with their ideas and plans. Having waited until the initial team became involved will provide the leaders with evidence of the feasibility of the project, should the superintendent object that teachers wouldn't participate. Depending on the relationship the leaders have with the superintendent, this step might be taken as the second step. In any event, it will be important to discuss the general outline of the project early on with the chief executive of the school system in order to get that person's initial clearance to begin additional discussions. The superintendent may want to discuss the project informally with some members of the school board or school council simply to let them know of the initial phase of the project, should someone go to them with questions. At this time the superintendent may want to assign a member of central office staff as liaison person with the school. This person would attend all major meetings and be kept informed, so that information is provided to the central office as the project develops. In any event, some regular process of communication should be set up at this time.

The Fourth Step

The leaders of the school can now begin conversations with small groups of parents. The most important message to get across is that parents are absolutely essential to the ethical development of their children. Introducing the project in general terms, the leaders will want to assure the parents that they are not seeking to replace them or any other institution, but rather to seek ways to link up with them. They want to talk about what is possible, rather than the ideal.

No doubt, questions will arise about difficult and contested ethical topics such as abortion and sexual ethics. Rather than respond off the top of their heads, the school leaders should have worked out ahead of time a well reasoned response to questions such as these. They may wish to develop a policy that on certain controversial issues the school will simply provide information about the major conflicting points of view and encourage the youngsters to talk with their parents as they try to develop where they will take their own stand. On other issues, such as racism, substance abuse, violence and sexism, the school may take a clear cut stand. The school leaders should try to point to the large ethical qualities of autonomy, connectedness and transcendence on which the school will be focusing. These are ethical qualities with which few parents will disagree.

These conversations will serve several purposes. First they will send a clear signal to the parents that the school wants their involvement and their ideas. They will also provide a useful information base upon which to build subsequent communications such as newsletters, progress reports, etc. about this ambitious project. In the course of these discussions with parents, school leaders should try to identify parents who might be particularly helpful in serving on committees later on in the process. It will make it easier to enlist their participation since they have been included early on. It will also provide the school leaders with some information about which parents should *not* be included on these committees, either because they are excessively intolerant of any point of view other than their own, because they give indications that they are not team players, or because they might launch their own moral crusade.

The Fifth Step

Depending on the circumstances, it may be appropriate to begin conversations with students at this point especially in the case of middle school, junior high school or senior high school students. Again, a more general discussion in their terminology of the moral problematics of the school would be appropriate, with discussions of directions they would like to see the school take. As with the parents, these discussions may reveal some potential leaders among the students who could serve on subsequent committees.

All the while these meetings are going on — with the superintendent, with parents and with students — the initial committee of teachers would be kept informed of developments. Some, or all of them may have been involved in these meetings. Their suggestions about carrying out these initiatives may prove very helpful. The results of these preliminary discussions should then be sifted and analyzed by the committee and, assuming that the signals are reasonably positive, a strategy for launching the formal opening of the project worked out. Those strategies would probably include steps similar to the ones listed below.

The Sixth Step

The project should be formally launched with the formation of a steering committee. The steering committee will be responsible for seeing the project through to the final stages of implementation, so they should be chosen carefully and with a view to the long haul. The committee could be made up of twelve people, with a representation of teachers, parents and students. Some would insist that the principal sit on the committee, others would, for equally strong reasons, insist that the principal not be on the committee. The principal and the initial *ad hoc* committee should discuss what seems best and decide. A reasonable representation on the steering committee would be five teachers, four parents, two students and the principal, or six teachers, if the principal does not sit on the committee. Members of the initial *ad hoc* committee of teachers should serve on the steering committee unless for some reason one or more choose not to.

The steering committee should take enough time at the outset to discuss the goals of the project perhaps taking up the ethical qualities it wants to promote in its students. They should also now begin a more formal discussion of the moral problematics of the school and the strengths that currently exist upon which they can build their ethical school. They may need time to delve more deeply into foundational ideas in the ethics of justice, the ethics of care, and the ethics of critique, or in other schools of thought that touch upon ethical education. Again, they need not thoroughly master the field of ethical theory. They will learn much as they get more involved in the project.

The Seventh Step

The steering committee should then begin to design the overall process the community will follow to build an ethical school. This involves elements necessary in both the initiation stage and the implementation stage. The initiation stage would be made up of preliminary discussions of foundational ideas, the self-study the community would engage in to identify those areas of strength and weakness in their present programs, initial designs of modifications in these programs, and necessary staff development as well as student and parent preparation workshops prior to implementation efforts.

The implementation stage would be made up of a phased, step by step series of activities by which the project would become operational, with a monitoring system to detect problems, a set of agreements about who was responsible for what, perhaps some vertical and horizontal communication and reporting arrangements, and some timetable for at least preliminary evaluation of the results of the changes.

For both the initiation and implementation stages, there will be four major working committees, responsible for dealing with ethical education in 1) the home, 2) the school curriculum, 3) the enrichment program, and 4) the institutional support systems. Some preliminary budget estimates for both the initiation and implementation stages should be projected (for example, for any teacher substitutes for teachers attending meetings, for preliminary workshops, for work during summers by design committees, etc.). All of these plans should be reviewed with central office staff and approval to move ahead secured.

The Eighth Step

After careful planning for the event, the steering committee should hold a meeting with the whole faculty and explain the project thoroughly, leaving time to answer initial questions and objections. Some kind of preliminary plans to carry out the project can be provided in writing at this time. In its presentation, the committee should point out and praise the work already being done at the school in ethical education. In this way the teachers will not perceive the project as a condemnation of their failure to deal with ethics. The committee might want to point to one or two areas that are ripe for development, or where an ethical focus could easily be added.

The teachers will need time to discuss the project among themselves, so a second meeting should be scheduled to canvass the results of their deliberations. Whether or not the steering committee will want to ask for a vote on whether to proceed with the project is a question to be decided at each school. In some cases, the assumption will be made that the project is simply so self-evidently called for that a positive response of the teachers can be assumed (although this does not preclude the possibility of some strong opposition by some teachers). In other cases, the style of faculty participation in school policy decisions may require a formal vote on the part of the teachers. In any event, the steering committee should communicate that teachers' recommendations and suggestions are welcomed and will be taken seriously, and that faculty participation will be absolutely essential for success.

The Ninth Step

Assuming that the teachers endorse the project, the steering committee, or a representative delegation from the committee should meet with the school board to discuss their plans. Prior to that meeting, the chair person of the board might have been briefed and his or her support solicited. Initial endorsement by the school board (or other governing body) would be essential.

The Tenth Step

Assuming that the board gives approval for launching the project, the steering committee should then hold one or more meetings with the parents in order to explain the project and to seek their participation and support. As was done in the preliminary discussions with parents, it should be made clear that the school is not seeking to supplant the role of parents and religious authorities in providing ethical guidance to the children. Rather, the school seeks to link up with them in order to reinforce a broad-based concern for the young people's growth in character and ethical sensitivity. Again, some statement of the goals of the project and some explanation of the planning process should be provided in writing. Depending on the politics of parental involvement, the officers of the home–school association may have been briefed earlier and their participation solicited, so that they might speak on behalf of the project at the meeting. Parental participation on committees, however, should not be limited to the officers of the home–school association.

The Eleventh Step

The project can now be formally launched by the appointment of the four working committees who will carry on with the self-study and the design of modifications to the various programs of the school (as described in the following chapter). These committees will work under the direction of the steering committee, with a calendar of deadlines to be met and with a set of operating guidelines and communication channels clearly delineated. The steering committee should appoint an ombudsman who will help the committees work through problems internal to the committee or between committees. The chairpersons of the various committees will meet with the steering committee once a month, or however often seems called for, in order to keep everyone informed of the process. Some kind of periodic newsletter will keep the total faculty, the parents, students, central office and school board appraised of the progress of the project.

Summary

The above steps provide one way of working through the process of launching such an ambitious project. To some, the initial steps may seem unnecessarily tedious. However, it is best to take a more thorough approach at the beginning in order to make sure that ideas are shared among a broad constituency of the school community before the project is actually launched. With a project this complex, it is necessary to develop stakeholders, people who will own the project and commit the necessary time and effort to see it through. Moreover, the initial structuring of the project should reflect the very ethical values the project seeks to promote — a sense of autonomy, connectedness and transcendence. By bringing the initial vision of the possibility of an ethical school to a broad constituency, the leaders of the school communicate a respect for the ideas of others, a trust in their sense of ethical values, a commitment to teamwork, and a commitment to honest participation. If that requires a longer investment of time at the outset, it is an investment that will pay rich dividends.

Note

1 For some readings on this important topic, see Ashton, P. and Webb, R. (1986) *Making a Difference: Teachers' Sense of Efficacy and Student Achievement*, New York, Longmans; Lieberman, A. (Ed.) (1988) *Building a Professional Culture in Schools*, New York, Teachers College Press; Maeroff, G. (1988) *The Empowerment of Teachers*, New York, Teachers College Press; Sarason, S. (1971) *The Culture of School and the Problem of Change*, Boston, Allyn and Bacon.

Chapter 7

Building an Ethical School: Designing a Plan

This chapter continues the outline of the initiation phase of the process of building an ethical school. Again, this does not represent the only way of building an ethical school. Rather, it illustrates in some detail how one process might work out. Local circumstances may dictate an alternative process. This chapter outlines how the working committees, under the guidance of the steering committee, engage in a self-study and, based on that, how they design possible new learning activities to enable that school more intentionally to engage in ethical education. The chapter goes on to explore possible phased implementation plans and concludes with a possible time frame for this initiation phase.

The Working Committees

Once the various working committees have been formed, they should spend some time in workshops and seminars where the larger, foundational ideas are presented (for example, the moral problematics of the school, the qualities of an ethical person, the three ethical frameworks). They should have adequate time to read some idea papers, discuss them and explore implications for their school.

Let us assume that four working committees have been formed, one to deal with ethical learnings in the home and neighborhood, one with the academic program, one with the enrichment or extra-curricular program, and one with the institutional support systems. If we are concerned with a relatively small elementary school, the academic committee may ask clusters of grade-level teachers to form subcommittees to do the preliminary work of the self-study. If we are talking about a school with academic departments, then the academic committee may request specific members of the staff to form subcommittees to deal with specific departmental programs, such as separate subcommittees to deal with language arts, social studies, sciences and the arts. Similarly, in a school with an extensive extra-curricular program, the working committee on the enrichment program (extra-curriculars) may need to request specific members of the staff to work on subcommittees in their areas. Likewise, the committee on institutional support may wish to divide the work among subcommittees dealing with guidance, special education placement procedures, grading/assessment and reward procedures, grievance and arbitration procedures, school discipline, etc. The committee on home learnings should be made up of current parents and perhaps one school faculty member.

The committee on home learning may want to divide into two or three subcommittees, one subcommittee for every two or three grade levels, so that ideas and suggestions may be targeted at children of different developmental stages. These subcommittees should start off discussing what kinds of ethical principles or themes they stress in the home and how they go about teaching ethical lessons to their children. These learnings should be summarized and the summary saved for a booklet which might be put together for other parents to consider in subsequent meetings or in their own homes. They might try out some exercises in which they take the three foundational qualities of autonomy, connectedness and transcendence and list three to five things they might do to nurture growth in these qualities in the home and in the neighborhood (see Figure 7.1). Next, committee members should brainstorm among themselves concerning the ethical lessons they think their children should be learning at school. Once they have created a sizeable list, they should then prioritize the items on the list into those that are most important and those less important. They should be encouraged to suggest practical learning activities which the teachers could devise for their children.

These suggestions should be added to the earlier summary of common ethical learnings supported in the home and presented to the steering committee. The steering committee should study the report of the committee on home learning and discuss with them any sections which might need modification or clarification. Assuming the report is approved, the steering committee should recommend the publication of the report of the committee on home learning for distribution to the board of education, to the teachers and to the parents at large.

The committee on home learning and its subcommittees will be a crucial vehicle for outreach and support for the parents. As they gain

Home Learnings

Autonomy	*Connectedness*	*Transcendence*
conversations about self-esteem and responsibility	experiences with extended family	learning conflict-resolution skills
doing chores around the house	having friends in the home	buying gifts for siblings
managing an allowance and a bank account	family oral history	volunteering for special helping activities in the home

Neighborhood Learnings

Autonomy	*Connectedness*	*Transcendence*
standing up to one's peers	membership in various groups (Boys Club, YWCA, Girl Scouts, 4-H Clubs, YMHA, etc.)	helping in various neighborhood projects (e.g., cleaning up a local park)
using one's special talents to help others		volunteer work at local hospital or soup kitchen
		visiting shut-ins

Figure 7.1: Mapping of possible home and neighborhood learnings

more experience with the project, they can take charge of such things as newsletters to parents or running workshops for parents who want to find out how to influence the ethical growth of their children. The committee can also generate monthly suggestions for activities in the home and neighborhood, suggestions which could be included in the newsletter, and which would complement what the school is try-ing to do that month. Over the course of two or three years, these sug-gestions might be collated and edited to form a workbook that parents in subsequent years might use.

The steering committee should instruct the three working com-mittees (and their subcommittees) dealing with the school-based learnings to conduct a self-study. The various subcommittees would look at what they are currently doing which supports the ethical growth of their students. A subcommittee might, for example, focus on the foundational qualities which the steering committee has identified as central to the school's effort (for example, autonomy, connectedness and transcendence) and then see how they *presently* nurture those val-ues or qualities in their curriculum/instructional activity. They should be able to point to specific learning activities in which the students engage, rather than the moral and sometimes 'preachy' messages teach-ers convey to students, for it is in specific and repeated activities that

	What Is		
	Autonomy	**Connectedness**	**Transcendence**
Language Arts	public speaking on their future careers writing their own poems critiques of characters in stories	cooperative learning writing stories about interpersonal problems	studies of heroes and heroines
Science		cooperative learning in science experiments	
Social Studies		learning the history of their grandparents comparing other cultures to their own	
Art Music	drawing a self-portrait composing their own songs playing musical instruments	drawing a family portrait	holiday concert for senior citizens

Figure 7.2: Worksheet for subcommittee in small elementary school, fourth grade

students will develop those values and qualities, rather than by listening to sermons by teachers.

After reviewing and listing the activities presently found in the programs, the subcommittee should then write out three to five additional learning activities which could be implemented in their program. These activities do not have to be add-ons; rather, they can use existing learning activities to teach simultaneously both an ethical lesson as well as an academic lesson. The subcommittees should be cautioned not to overburden their programs with ethical learning activities. A carefully crafted selection of quality learnings will go a long way when they are interwoven with learning activities from other programs into a rich tapestry that expresses the efforts of all three areas of school life: the academic program, the enrichment program, and the institutional supports. The subcommittees might be able to summarize their deliberations through the use of work sheets such as those in Figures 7.2 and 7.3. Similar deliberations could take place in subcommittees dealing with extra-curriculars, as is illustrated in Figure 7.4.

In addition, those subcommittees should also engage in discussions concerning the use of the three ethical frameworks of justice, care and critique to develop sensitivity to ethical issues in their specific

	What Could Be Added		
	Autonomy	**Connectedness**	**Transcendence**
Language Arts	more creative writing exercises debate exercises on public issues	acting out stories in class and then sharing feelings about the character one played writing family histories	writing letters to the editor of the local paper writing letters to pen pals in another country writing letters to people in prison
Science	inviting an extra-credit activity of inventing something and explaining it to the class	working on a team science project for the science fair	contacting a local environmental club about environmental problems
Social Studies	Making a map of their neighborhood and its history	studying the effects of malnutrition in early childhood	studying the causes of and solutions to world famine
Art/Music	draw a picture of a favorite thing sing or play a favorite song	draw a picture of a good friend draw a picture as a gift to one of your parents make tape recording of five songs for your grandparents	create 12 greeting cards to send to shut-ins make a poster for school spirit day

Figure 7.3: Mapping suggestions for new learning activities in the fourth grade of a small school

	What Is					
	Soccer	*Volleyball*	*Track*	*Basketball*	*Baseball*	*Softball*
Autonomy	learning to master the skills necessary to compete in the game					
Connectedness	learning teamwork, school spirit, school traditions					
Transcendence	making sacrifices for the sake of the team and for the school; upholding a code of conduct and a code of honor for athletes; living up to principles of fair play and good sportsmanship					
	What Could Be Added					
Autonomy Connectedness	Do all of the present things in the program with greater attention and concentration by the coaches.					
Transcendence	Involve varsity athletes in Special Olympics for handicapped children; in big brother, big sister programs in conjunction with the guidance department; in coaching intramural teams.					

Figure 7.4: Worksheet for a subcommittee on boys' and girls' interscholastic athletics

What Is

Subject Area: *Eleventh Grade Social Studies (American History)*

Justice	Discussion of principles of justice: a) justifying the American Revolutionary War b) in the treatment of Native Americans by the US government c) in the US Constitution as a social contract
Care	
Critique	Discussion of assumptions behind slavery Discussion of assumptions behind prohibition

What Could Be Added

Justice	studies of the labor movement, of women's suffrage, of reform of the welfare system
Care	discussion of government policies dealing with health, child protection, the homeless and mentally ill
Critique	discussions of discrimination in various forms (race, sex, religion, ethnicity); discussion of American defense policy in last thirty years

Figure 7.5: Worksheet summarizing the use of ethical perspectives in academic subcommittee

areas. Whereas learning activities dealing with the foundational qualities provide the unspoken ground for all ethical education, attention to specific ethical questions derived from the three ethics of justice, care and critique help to develop expressly ethical habits of thinking in which explicit questions of responsibility and obligation can be considered. Figure 7.5 suggests a way to record such activities.

The various subcommittees should then meet with their working committee and share their reports. They should be asked to note areas where they could engage in some cross disciplinary or cross grade linkages or networking, where they might use older students to help with the learning activities of the younger students, etc. These areas of complementarity should be noted in their report to their respective committees.

Each working committee should review the data and look for clusters of strength in existing programs and for clusters of suggested learning activities which tend to support and complement each other. They should then draw up an overview summary report, perhaps on forms similar to those contained in Figures 7.6 through 7.11, containing summaries of those foundational qualities and ethical frameworks currently supported in the school's programs (or, as the case may be, contradicted by the school's practice), as well as summaries of suggestions for improving their support of the foundational qualities and

What Is
A Discipline System of Control through Sanctions, Grades 9–12

Autonomy	Learns that actions have consequences; rules apply to all; learns to accept punishment for violating the rules; learns to follow the rules
Connectedness	learns ambivalence, if not antagonism, toward those in authority
Transcendence	

What Could Be Added
A Developmental Discipline System that Moves from External Control to Internal Self-Governance

Autonomy	Discipline Office, with Guidance Office conducts a series of group discussions with students about self-respect, resisting crowd influence, about non-violent ways of resolving conflicts. Discipline Office, with Art Department makes and displays posters carrying themes of self-respect, integrity, community and responsibility.
Connectedness	Student learns that there is an authority higher than him/herself: the community; learns that the community must govern itself for its own good; learns to deal with the ambivalence of wanting his/her own way and wanting to belong. Discipline Office, with Guidance Department, conducts an ongoing series of discussions on multicultural plurality within community.
Transcendence	Student learns to negotiate with authorities for both autonomous as well as community initiatives. Discipline office trains student conflict-resolution teams; uses big brother/big sister program for follow-through with those having discipline problems; student government to have greater say in school discipline policies.

Figure 7.6: Summary worksheet for school disciplinary system

ethical frameworks. These summary reports are then submitted in both oral and written form to the steering committee.

Overview by the Steering Committee

The steering committee may now add the reports of the school working committees to the report of the home learning committee in order to gain an overview of the present activities of the school and the home in ethical education, as well as an overview of the possibilities for additional school-wide and home learnings. It would be helpful if the committee could identify complementary elements of strength among current practices in each of the four areas of home learnings, academics, institutional supports and enrichment programs. These could be connected perhaps by common themes.

The committee should also look for similar relationships among

What Is

A Discipline System of Control through Sanctions, Grades 9–12

Justice	Student learns that rules apply to all; experiences punishment for violation of rules; learns that rules are made by authorities; that he/she has no say in changing them.
Care	Student learns to take care of him/herself by avoiding detection.
Critique	Student learns to debate the application of a rule and the legitimacy of the rule itself.

What Could Be Added

A Developmental Discipline System that Moves from External Control to Internal Self-Governance

Justice	Student moves from feeling dominated by a social contract that he/she had no say in, to gradual participation in various processes of self-governance, especially through student government representation. All classroom rules set by both the teacher and the class.
Care	Student handbook stresses caring and community more than rules, or as a basis for what rules there are. Discipline Office, with Guidance Department, conducts seminars on self-respect and group responsibility.
Critique	Student encouraged to critique the way things work at school, and to express opinions to and through the student government; participation on conflict resolution teams provides some opportunity to explore alternatives to the status quo.

Figure 7.7: Additional summary worksheet on school discipline

Guidance Department, Grades 9–12

What Is

Autonomy	Conversations with students about self-esteem.
Connectedness	Conversations with students about friendship, sex, parents, careers, groups and gangs.
Transcendence	Conversations with students about careers, hobbies.

What Could Be Added

Autonomy	Guidance Department (GD) conducts group seminars on self-esteem, self-respect, taking responsibility for oneself. GD conducts workshop for teachers on importance of self-esteem.
Connectedness	GD sponsors group seminars on multicultural plurality, avoidance of stereotyping, and on conflict-resolution; promotes big brother/big sister program; collaborates with Discipline Office on building healthier sense of community.
Transcendence	GD works with Discipline Office to train student conflict-resolution teams.

Figure 7.8: Summary worksheet of high school guidance department

Guidance Department, Grades 9–12

What Is

Justice	Guidance Department (GD) helps negotiate reconciliation after fights in school and at home.
Care	GD models caring adults.
Critique	

What Could Be Added

Justice	GD runs a seminar for faculty on adolescents' stages of cognitive moral development. GD conducts study of imbalance of minorities and ESL students in Special Education classifications. GD and Special Education teachers conduct seminars on mainstreaming.
Care	GD runs group seminars for students and teachers on overcoming stereotyping. GD participates in planning various multicultural activities. GD speaks out for Special Education students whose mainstreaming experience is totally negative.
Critique	GD works with Discipline Office to overhaul school discipline program. GD works on improving Special Education placements. GD conducts seminars for seniors and juniors on lifestyle and career choices as a way of opening up considerations about life values.

Figure 7.9: Additional summary worksheet for high school guidance department

the suggested learning activities in each of the four areas. Having identified them, they might think about building specific plans around these activities that share such relationships. The steering committee should then prepare a summary report of the self-study to be distributed to the school board or council, to the teachers and to the parents. Since the steering committee will have to summarize and display a large amount of information in this report, it might be helpful to use coded summary worksheets similar to those found in Figures 7.12 and 7.13.

Designing Possibilities for Implementation

While the overview report is being drafted, the steering committee should begin discussions concerning an implementation plan. When they present the overview report to the faculty, they should be prepared to offer several possible designs for implementation of the suggestions of the self-study. As they think about implementing the numerous suggestions which the subcommittees have made, they should project alternative phasing-in possibilities. For example, they should

Enrichment Programs

What Is

	Autonomy	Connectedness	Transcendence
Clubs	learns mastery of skills, competence, self-expression	learns cooperation, makes friends	learns about striving for excellence; connects with something larger than self
Varsity Athletics	learns mastery of skills	makes friends	learns honor code, discipline and sacrifice
Community Service		makes friends	learns sacrifice; gratification of serving others
Student Government	makes a contribution; learns responsibility	learns school pride; experiences community	learns sacrifice for good of community

What Could Be Added

	Autonomy	Connectedness	Transcendence
Clubs		clubs provide community service	clubs provide community service
Varsity Athletics			work with Special Olympics; coach intramurals; participate in big brother/big sister program
Community Service	learns to keep a journal		
Student Government			works with big brother/big sister program

Figure 7.10: Summary worksheet for high school enrichment program

consider implementing improvements in all four areas of home learnings, academics, institutional supports, and enrichment, but over a three year period. In the first year the committee would target approximately one-third of the suggested learning activities for implementation, especially those activities which might have some relationships across all four areas. By not taking on the whole improvement effort in one year, they would have a chance to try out a limited number of new activities, probably dealing with the less complex ethical topics, to see how they worked out. Building on their experience with the first year, the committee could then in the second year work on a second set of suggested learning activities, perhaps those that are a little more complex, and in the third year a third set.

Another option would be to think of a three year implementation phase-in, but now according to each of the school areas. In the first

Enrichment Program, Grades 9–12

What Is

	Justice	Care	Critique
Clubs	learns rules of membership		
Varsity Athletics	learns fair play		
Community Service		learns to care for others	sees how people are stereotyped
Student Government	learns rules of self-governance	learns to care for others	learns how to name shortcomings of school and to negotiate for change

What Could Be Added

	Justice	Care	Critique
Clubs		engaged in community service	
Varsity Athletics		Special Olympics; big brother/big sister program	discussions of competitive pressures on athletes
Community Service	studies rights of people being served		evaluates agencies that serve clients; seeks improvements
Student Government	supports developmental discipline program	participates in big brother/big sister program	seeks evaluation of student government performance; speaks to school board once each year about student concerns

Figure 7.11: Additional summary worksheet for high school enrichment program

year the committee might tackle the enrichment activities, the second year the institutional support programs and in the third year the academics. Such a plan would allow maximum time for the teachers to work on the implementation plans for the academics, which may prove the most complicated. The home learnings could be responding to the school learnings being highlighted in each year.

A third option would be based on the premise that academic work is the area requiring greatest attention. This option would target specific grades for implementing the academic learnings during the first year, additional grades in the second year and the rest of the grades in the third year. The home learnings, enrichment and institutional support activities could be phased on a more *ad hoc* basis, depending on the priorities of the staff.

Foundational Qualities Academic Program Support

What Is

	Autonomy	Connectedness	Transcendence
First Grade	CM A LA HL HL	LA CM A CL CL	
Second Grade	CM LA LA CM HL	CL CL CL LA CM	
Third Grade	CM HL CM HL LA	LA SS CL	
Fourth Grade	LA HL LA HL LA	CL LA M HL	HL LA
Fifth Grade	CM HL CM HL HL LA	SI SS SI SS LA CM	CM HL

What Could Be Added

	Autonomy	Connectedness	Transcendence
First Grade	A HL A HL CM	A A CM	A A
Second Grade	A HL A HL	SS	A
Third Grade	LA HL LA HL A	SS SS	A
Fourth Grade	A HL A HL LA	A LA M SI SS SS	A
Fifth Grade	A HL LA HL LA	CL HL SS HL SI	SI A HL HL HL

Key: A = Art; CM = Classroom Management; CL = Cooperative Learning; HL = Home-based Learning; M = Music/Chorale; LA = Language Arts;
SI = Science; SS = Social Studies

Figure 7.12: Steering committee summary worksheet of academic program support of foundational qualities

Ethical Frameworks Academic Program Support

What Is

	Justice	Care	Critique
First Grade	CM CM	CM CL — HL HL	
Second Grade	CM CM	CM CM — HL HL	
Third Grade	CM CM — LA	A CM — HL HL	
Fourth Grade	CM SS	A CM CL — HL HL	
Fifth Grade	CM CM CM — LA	A — HL HL	

What Could Be Added

	Justice	Care	Critique
First Grade	CM CM	CL	
Second Grade	LA CM	CM CM CL — HL	
Third Grade	LA — HL HL	CM LA LA — HL CL	
Fourth Grade	LA SS SS — LA HL	CL LA LA — HL HL A M	SS
Fifth Grade	SS SS SS — CM CM HL	CL CL LA — HL HL A	SS SI SS — HL HL

Key: A = Art; CL = Cooperative Learning; CM = Classroom Management; HL = Home-based Learning; LA = Language Arts; M = Music/Chorale; SI = Science; SS = Social Studies

Figure 7.13: Steering committee summary worksheet of academic program support of ethical frameworks

Having discussed the pros and cons of alternative plans, and having analyzed the reports of the subcommittees to gain a school-wide perspective of the strengths and suggested areas for improvement, the steering committee should now call a meeting of the whole teaching staff to summarize the progress to date. At the meeting with the teachers, the steering committee should discuss the options open to them for organizing an implementation plan. They would discuss with the teachers the apparent advantages of one plan over another, and ask for their feedback. The steering committee should allow the teachers adequate time to discuss the advantages and disadvantages of various implementation plans. After an appropriate time for discussion (perhaps a week or two), they may want to ask for a vote on which implementation plan they prefer. The steering committee should at least attempt to gauge the sentiments of the faculty at this point.

The steering committee would then send the summary report of the self-study to the parents and to the school board or council. At meetings with the parents they should encourage parental comments on the self-study. Again, the connection between ethical lessons in the home and neighborhood and the ethical lessons learned in school should be emphasized. These meetings should intentionally aim at building a sense of collaboration and teamwork between the home and the school.

A presentation of the findings of the self-study should also be made to the school board or council. If possible, some visible sign of support should be requested at this point, since the parents and teachers will need encouraging words from those in authority to continue the effort. It might be entirely appropriate for the school board or council to authorize a modest sum for an end-of-year party or picnic that would honor the work of the various committees, inviting students, parents and teachers to enjoy a celebration of their accomplishments.

Designing the First Phase of Implementation

Let us assume, for the sake of developing the specifics of a planning process, that the faculty sentiment is in favor of the first option — implementing the suggested activities in all three areas, but over three years. The steering committee should then reconvene the three working committees and their subcommittees and review with them in a general session those activities which seem to be related across the four areas (perhaps connected by some common themes). The working committees should then meet individually with their subcommittees to select those learning activities which they think most suitable for the first phase of implementation. When they have made their selection, the working committees should meet together to see where they have chosen learnings that mutually reinforce one another. These discussions among working committees may require further adjustments in their choices in order to coordinate the chosen learnings across all four areas. Whenever possible, they should try to lay out a calendar of when these learnings might take place during the school year, so that they might construct a developmentally appropriate sequence of learnings, which are reinforced in more than one of the four areas. When they have satisfied themselves that they have individually and collectively decided on a workable selection of learning activities for the first year of the implementation process, they should submit their reports to the steering committee.

The steering committee reviews the reports of the working committees to check for excessive overlap, excessive crowding of the existing curriculum with an overabundance of new learnings, as well as to note and reinforce the learnings that mutually reinforce each other. The steering committee then puts together a plan for the first year of implementation. This plan contains a calendar of the sequence of the various learnings throughout the year for each grade level in the school. Perhaps using a color code, the plan will indicate learnings which support the development of the foundational qualities of autonomy, connectedness and transcendence, as well as those learnings which apply the ethic of justice, the ethic of care, or the ethic of critique. This master plan is then sent out to the parents, the teachers, and the school board or council. This plan will constitute the agenda for the summer workshops of the teachers and parents who will work for two weeks or more to flesh out the details of the learning activities which the four working committees have chosen.

End of Year Events

The end of the school year should be punctuated by a festive party. Parents, students and teachers should come together to enjoy music and dancing and awards. The superintendent and chairperson of the board or council should speak of the significance of the work accomplished and of the promise that lies ahead. Various chairpersons of the working committees and of the steering committee should be commended, and special awards given out to those who made special contributions to the year's work.

When the summer holidays begin, there is yet more work to do. The four working committees should come together with their sub-committees and attempt to flesh out the details of the learning activities. This would include identifying necessary resources, antecedent workshops for teachers and students, reading material, suggested assessment activities, a schedule, the person(s) to be accountable for implementation, a monitoring process and reporting of achievements. Whenever the subcommittees feel the need to consult with any particular member of the staff not on that committee, they should do so in order to utilize the full expertise of the staff. The subcommittees should also feel free to check with colleagues teaching in other schools or with various professional associations of teachers and subject matter specialists while they are doing this design work. There are many educators involved in a variety of attempts at ethical education who can be contacted for help. Some of these sources are mentioned in Appendix I of this book.

Designing Assessments

After they have designed the learning activities, the working committees should be asked to prepare end-of-semester assessments of the learning that resulted from the various learning activities. These assessments might take the form of a reflective essay which responds to an ethical case study or a variety of simulated ethical challenges and role playing responses to them. However the assessments are constructed the committees should try to make them 'authentic', that is, assessments which require responses that closely mirror the expected responses in the learning activities themselves. Let us suppose that one of the themes treated in several learning activities in the semester dealt with keeping promises or honoring agreements or contracts. The assessment should place the student in a situation where it will be difficult to hold to a promise or an agreement, where the rewards for breaking an agreement are very tempting, or the consequences for not breaking a promise are quite negative. Not only should the student be forced to decide what to do, but, once the choice is made, the student must explain why that particular choice was made, how it respected the rights of and loyalties to the parties involved, how it expressed or violated his or her own sense of integrity, how the choice represented or violated a principle in which the student believed. Assuming that the students had been exposed to these kinds of exercises during their learning activities, the assessment should indicate how those learning activities have prepared or influenced the student to respond.

The topic of assessment raises some very sensitive questions. Can a student fail an assessment of ethical learning? If we are consistent, we have to say that, yes, a student can fail such an assessment. In other words, if the community believes that honoring agreements and keeping promises are ethical and that violating them, *unless there is a higher principle or obligation involved*, is unethical, then a student who, in an assessment performance, violates a promise or agreement has failed the test. Where the student perceives a higher principle or obligation to be involved and can explain what that is, then he or she should be considered as having passed the test, for that is, in fact, the ethical choice to be made.

The assessments should avoid highly controversial ethical issues, for example, the issue of abortion, for clearly the community is divided on such problems. This does not mean that a controversial ethical problem cannot be discussed in class, with students being exposed to the arguments which various opposing groups put forth to bolster their claim for ethical righteousness. To make these problems the subject of an end of semester assessment, however, appears inappropriate because of the judgments that must be made about passing and failing.

Let us assume, however, that some students fail some rather straightforward ethical performance assessments. A conference with the parents would seem in order as a first step. Assuming that the parent wants to pursue the matter, both the home and school can pursue various remediation efforts, depending on their diagnosis of where the problem lies. Nevertheless, most veteran educators would agree that there will be some youngsters who will defy all efforts at remediation, and one may be left with having to live with one or two 'impossible cases'.

As with grading in the more regular academic subjects, what is important is the learning and, where problems are apparent, the remediated learning. Sometimes, we teach the opposite lesson by making a fetish of the grades rather than seeing them as helpful, but not absolute, measures of learning.

Putting the Smaller Plans into Bigger Plans

When each subcommittee completes its plan for the first year of implementation, it is submitted to the corresponding working committee, which then creates a more comprehensive, coordinated plan of activities for the relevant area, whether that be academics, home, enrichment or institutional supports. The working committees should take care that the learning activities are concentrated, high quality learning experiences. Here the principle of 'less is more' should be considered. The point is not, especially in the first year, to present the students and teachers with a blizzard of ethical learning activities, but a select, well-designed few activities which make their point clearly. When these learning activities are joined to learning activities in the other three areas, there will be more than enough time spent during the school year on ethical lessons.

The working committees then pass on their plans to the steering committee. The steering committee studies the plans and seeks to connect, where possible, elements of the plans which complement each other. The steering committee then coordinates the work of the four working committees into a final school-wide plan for the first year of implementation. This plan would contain a month-by-month calendar of activities so that both teachers and parents can cross-reference what is happening in various programs and support them more intentionally. This would also assist monitoring procedures, once the implementation is underway. It may turn out that the preliminary calendar will be modified as the plans are put into practice. Nevertheless, it can serve as a model for what should be available, month by month, to everyone on the staff, and to the parents, once the first stage of implementation is begun. The calendar will probably be incomplete, since on any given day, a teacher or parent may find an unexpected but very appropriate occasion to engage the students in ethical considerations. The calendar, however, will normally provide basic information helpful to coordinating efforts by parents and various members of the staff.

Review of Teachers and Parents

The final school-wide plan for the first year of implementation is then sent to the teachers, the principal, the superintendent and the board. It should contain a supplementary budget for the plan; indicate a calendar which expresses the timing of new activities; highlight any staff development needs; and outline ongoing evaluation and administrative monitoring processes.

At this point the involvement of the whole teaching staff should be fairly complete, so the report of the steering committee should come as no surprise. It will be important, however, for every teacher to have a sense of what others are expected to be doing while that teacher is working on his or her own learning activities. Everyone needs to feel a part of a concerted community effort, as well as to be able to connect various learning activities with what is going on elsewhere in the school and in the home.

Highlights of the Initiation Process

At this point the school appears ready to engage in the first phase of the school-wide effort at ethical education. It may be helpful here to pause and highlight the features of this suggested initiation phase of the process.

The process began with a small team of teachers who were willing to explore the idea of building an ethical school. They initially had to spend time reading and discussing some foundational ideas around which they could frame various possibilities for a more intentional school-wide effort at ethical education. They then did an informal assessment of what kind of ethical education was currently evident in the present activities of the school. Their early discussions opened up to include parents, central office administrators and then a larger group of the faculty. During these initial discussions, the process was very open-ended, seeking out ideas that came from participants, communicating a desire for full participation from various sectors.

A steering committee and four working teams were assigned to carry out the self-study and design the plans. As the process became more formalized, communications with various sectors on a regular basis became important. Progress reports, newsletters, strategic meetings for face-to-face discussion with various groups were all essential to keep everyone informed and involved. Internal as well as external support was important. When appropriate, budgetary considerations were raised and approval sought.

Once the preliminary plans were formulated and discussed, specific responsibilities for teachers and parents and administrators became more apparent. Systems of communication, of accountability, of assessment and evaluation became more formalized. Those to be most directly involved in the implementation of the effort were now involved in designing the specific ways they would participate. In other words, responsibility for doing the work was coupled with the design of the work itself, in that way maximizing ownership of the effort.

Another important aspect of the initiation process was an effort to integrate ethical education with already existing programs. Rather than creating a new program which might require additional teachers and substantial new funding, the process sought to link up with current academic and enrichment programs and develop the ethical material already embedded in those programs. The process also sought to develop a few ethical learning activities of high quality, rather than overwhelming existing programs with a multiplicity of ethical lessons. These few quality learning activities, however, would be connected with other learning activities in other areas, both in enrichment programs and in institutional support activities, so that the learnings could be reinforced in various settings.

Finally, the role of parents and family was continually emphasized. The school programs had to be working in cooperation with the efforts at home. The parents are the primary ethical educators in a young person's life. The school has to join its efforts with the parents and work in partnership.

Time Frames

What kind of time blocks will such a process involve? It is important to recognize that while all the activities of the initiation phase are going on, the school is functioning within its normal schedule of activities. Daily classes, grading of homework and quizzes, parent conferences, yard and cafeteria duties, staff meetings, assemblies, fire drills, science and art fairs, interscholastic and intramural athletics — the whole circus is in full swing. Hence the process has to respect the limited energies and time left over for the additional work involved in the initiation phase. The process also has to respect the rhythms of the school year. The end of semester and the end of school year are not the times to ask for extended, quality discussions. Usually the last month of each term or semester should be free from major work commitments of the initiation phase. Keeping these things in mind, then, what might a reasonable time frame look like? Figure 7.14 illustrates one proposed schedule.

Some might complain that this time frame is too long, that teachers and parents will not be able to sustain interest over such a long time. Yet, if one considers the many other demands on the staff during the regular school year, this two-year initiation phase of the process is crowded. Some schools may want to expand the time frame so as to provide the staff additional time to absorb and discuss the ideas and projected learning activities. The danger with providing a more leisurely time frame is that the process will lack sufficient intensity. There is something to be said for imposing somewhat stringent time demands

Year I	Year II
Previous Year and Summer Months	*Summer Workshops*
School leaders consider the prospect of building an ethical school, study the building blocks, etc., to launch the project.	Working committees meet with steering committee to set agenda; create a plan for the year; study foundational ideas, begin self-study.
Beginning of School Year	*Beginning of School Year*
Initial survey of present practices in ethical education; formation of initial teacher teams to discuss feasibility.	Working committees and their subcommittees continue self-study, identifying present attempts at ethical education.
Initial discussion with school authorities and informal discussion with parents and students.	Working committees collate data on present efforts at ethical education.
Reflection on initial discussions; decision to go forward; planning.	Working committees and subcommittees identify additional, potential learning activities.
	Working committees collate information and send reports to steering committee.
Mid-Year Holidays	*Mid-Year Party*
Formation of steering committee (SC); SC time to study foundational ideas and ethical frameworks; planning.	SC reviews reports and constructs a school-wide report.
Meetings with the board, teachers, and parents to outline the project and seek their involvement.	Parents and teachers receive report and study it; feedback and discussions of possible implementation plans; decision on implementation plan.
Assignment of working committees; they study foundational ideas and ethical frameworks. Planning of summer workshops.	Working committees and subcommittees choose learnings for first phase of implementation; coordination among three school areas; reports to steering committee.
	SC puts together a schoolwide plan, circulates it, and prepares for summer workshop
End of School Year	*End of Year Party*

Figure 7.14: A two-year schedule of the initiation phase

on a group. They will marshal the energy for short, intensive bursts of creative energy with better results than what a more drawn out process might produce.

At this point we are ready to move into the implementation phases. Now the fun begins, because teachers and parents will have a chance to put their plans into action.

Chapter 8

Building an Ethical School: Implementation Phases

The First Year of Implementation

After the work of the various committees has been summarized by the steering committee, everyone should take a well deserved holiday. During the summer, if not before, the school administration should appoint a project director, someone who will coordinate the school-wide effort during the implementation phase. That person might likely come from the steering committee. The project director and the administration should plan the first month of the school year very carefully.

The teachers should come in for the start of the school year two or three days before the students arrive. They will have received in advance the comprehensive school-wide plan sent out by the steering committee, so they will already have some idea of what is expected of them. During these initial days, the whole school staff should meet to review the plans for the semester and the year. The project director should explain what is expected of the individual staff members, whom to see if difficulties arise, and suggest ways to coordinate learning activities across disciplines and across other areas such as enrichment programs. The project director will also indicate the dates for teachers to review their progress in their working groups, point out the complementary efforts being expected from the parents, and indicate the kind of end-of-semester assessments of student learnings that will be utilized and the survey information from the parents that will be reviewed at the end of the semester.

As each teacher comes to terms with the implementation effort being asked, it may become apparent to some that they are going to need more specific help. This is where the leadership of those on the subcommittees who drew up the activities will come into play. Either on a one-to-one basis, or in small groups, they should be meeting with those teachers who need more clarification and direction. In some cases, attendance at a professional workshop may be called for. In any event, specific staff development days during the first month of school should be planned for this purpose. During the first month of the school year, the whole teaching faculty will be expected to make whatever last minute preparations for the start of the project are necessary. The first phase gets under way at the beginning of the second month of the school year.

During the first few weeks of school, the project director and the home learning committee present the plan to the parents at several afternoon and evening meetings. The home learning committee will indicate how the suggestions of learning activities for parents to follow at home would support and reflect the specific lessons being learned at school. They should encourage parents to discuss the new school initiatives with their children on a regular basis, to get a sense of what they are learning. The home learning committee should encourage parents to provide feedback to teachers and administrators about these conversations at home, for they may be the best sources for evaluative data on the impact of the new learnings. The parents should be told of the end-of-semester assessment survey of the parents' opinions about what their children are learning from the efforts at ethical education. Some of this information should also be sent in writing to the parents.

Managing the Logistics of Implementation

The implementation phase of the process differs considerably from the initiation phase of the process. In the initiation phase, the process was less formal, more open-ended, called upon creative responses from participants, was more consensual and authority was shared quite equally among participants. The implementation phase of the process, on the other hand, involves participants in following through on their agreements, according to agreed upon schedules and protocols. This is not the time for creative invention, for open-ended exploration of ideas; this is the time for action. Hence this phase of the process is more organized, more formal, less flexible. People are expected now to do what they agreed to do, according to the schedule they agreed upon, following the rules they set, using the appropriate communication and reporting channels.

There should be one person who functions as project director.

This person is responsible for many of the administrative and coordinating details of the implementation phase. The project director sees that everyone has the monthly calendar, checks with the teachers involved, puts up a weekly poster of learning activities and topics to be treated that week in the teachers' room so that everyone is reminded what is happening that week, and informally monitors how things are proceeding. The project director keeps a log of events so that there will be a record of how the implementation phase developed.

There should be a monthly calendar which charts when the learning activities are scheduled to take place. This calendar does not necessarily specify the exact day for each learning activity, but lists them by the weeks they are due to take place. Individual teachers will have some discretion in introducing specific learning activities, but they should see that they take place in the week assigned. The calendar may indicate a sequence of learning activities extending over three or four weeks, first in social studies, then in athletics, then in the guidance program, then in an assembly. By having the calendar, everyone on the staff is aware of what is being stressed that month. Other teachers in the school may want to reinforce these learnings or refer to them as it seems appropriate, for example, on the playground or in the lunchroom.

Every week there should be a large poster in the teachers' room indicating any special learning activities taking place that week. The poster might have a theme, or a quotation that embodies the theme, as a way to capture the teachers' attention.

Teachers should be asked, especially at the beginning, to keep some record of how their efforts are progressing. What are the successes, the surprises, the failures? What new ideas came up while attempting to teach that unit? Why did the youngsters respond the way they did? Where there are several teachers teaching the same grade level who will be engaged in teaching the same learning activity in the same week, they will be encouraged to share their results within two or three days after those attempts. These personal records will help the teachers in the reflection sessions they will be asked to engage in every four to six weeks during the implementation phase, so they can share their successes and problems with one another. In any event, major problems should be reported to the project director right away. Some teachers might fail badly in their first attempt and be tempted to give up on the whole effort. They need to be supported and coached into new efforts.

The parent committee will also be sending out, on a regular basis, suggestions of possible activities at home in which parents may involve their youngsters to complement what is being taught in school.

After the first month of the implementation, the parent committee will telephone a random sample of the parents to ask for their perception of how the new program is working and to see whether the parents are following through at home. The project director will work with the parent committee to construct a parent survey which will be sent out at the end of the semester to have parents evaluate how the school's efforts and their own are affecting their children. Initial drafts of the survey should be tried out on a sample of parents to see whether it is intelligible, and whether there are other items which should be included.

In the first month, the project director should also establish a student advisory committee of four to eight students who will take informal soundings of their peers on the impact of the new initiatives throughout the school. That advisory committee will meet every three or four weeks with the project director and perhaps with members of the steering committee to report on their perception of students' reactions to the initiatives.

It will be important for teachers to share stories of their successes and failures in these new efforts. No doubt there will be some spontaneous anecdotal sharing in the teachers' room. Nevertheless, the project director should schedule a session every four to six weeks in the first semester for teachers and staff to share more formal reports of how the work is progressing. What is working? What doesn't work? What needs shoring up? What needs to be dropped? All three working committees of the school-wide effort will need to engage in these reviews and report back to the steering committee. Likewise, the home committee will have to report their findings from telephone calls to random samples of parents concerning the efforts on the homefront. Teachers will also have gained some impression of the cooperation of the parents by talking with their students, and through the customary parent–teacher nights. The steering committee will take all this information and review it. It may then decide whether any adjustments or correctives are in order.

At the end of the semester student assessments of ethical learnings are administered and the results studied carefully by the teachers and reported to the steering committee. Likewise the parent survey will be administered and the results studied by the home committee and the project director and reported to the steering committee. The steering committee will process this information and prepare a set of recommendations for the teachers, staff and parents, recommendations which the steering committee will issue at the beginning of the second semester.

The First Year of Implementation, Second Semester

After the meeting called by the steering committee to review their end-of-semester report, the process carries on. The project director will continue to send out monthly calendars of scheduled learning activities to various sectors of the school community. The director will also continue displaying the weekly poster of scheduled activities in the teachers' room, so that those activities scheduled for that week will be fresh in everyone's mind. The director will also schedule the review sessions for the four working committees and their subcommittees every four to six weeks, and continue to meet with the student advisory committee to stay in touch with student sentiment.

The home committee will continue to send out a monthly list of suggested activities in the home and neighborhood which will complement the efforts being made at the school. The home committee will also continue their sampling of parental perceptions and involvement via telephone calls.

While all this is going on the steering committee will call together the working committees and invite them to begin work on designing the learning activities for the second phase of the implementation to be carried out the following year. The working committees and their subcommittees will keep in mind the assessments of the first semester and the recommendations of the steering committee, so that they can build on the experience gained in the first attempt at implementation. Again, the emphasis will be on choosing a few quality learning experiences in each of the four areas and seeking to link them according to themes or issues. The activities of the second phase should build on those of the first phase and deepen and expand the range of ethical concerns. The plans which they submit should include both the activities of the first phase and the new activities of the second phase, because new activities will be required, in addition to the activities of the first phase, for the coming year. By including the activities of previous years in each successive phase, by the final implementation phase, everyone will have a full picture of the variety of ethical learning activities that have been built into the curriculum.

The plans which the subcommittees and the four working committees prepare will make up the preliminary master plan for the second year. This master plan will be taken up in more detail during the summer when the teachers, staff and parents have the time to flesh them out and develop resource materials and assessments.

At the end of the second semester, student assessments and parent surveys are once again administered and their results studied carefully by the four committees and by the steering committee. At the beginning of the summer workshops, the steering committee will summarize the information and make recommendations. The steering committee should also at this time stage a big party or picnic which brings together parents, teachers and students to celebrate the year's achievements. This may be an occasion to recognize outstanding contributions from the parents, teachers, staff and students.

The Second Year of Implementation

The summer in between the first and second year of implementation will see the working committees and their subcommittees directing the whole faculty and staff in discussing the steering committee's end-of-year report, especially with a view to its implications for their work in the second year of implementation. Following these discussions, the faculty, staff and parent volunteers will begin work on the steering committee's master plan for the second year of implementation, fleshing out the initial designs of the second year activities, developing learning resources and materials, and constructing student assessments. The steering committee will take the work of the four working committees and construct a comprehensive master plan for the year. This plan will then be divided into monthly calendars of activities. Any staff development or parent workshops that anticipate the work of the coming year should also be provided for at this time. The summer might also be a time when counselors and social workers and other parents might work more intensively with families and students who are experiencing major difficulties with the program.

Beginning the Second Year

The second year of implementation will begin with a meeting of the whole faculty to review what everyone will be doing in all four areas. Similar meetings will be held for parents to communicate the same information and to enlist their continued support. In both cases it will be made clear that the second year's activities are being added to those initiated in the previous year (at least those that have survived evaluation). The project director will then see to the distribution of the monthly calendars to all parties involved, as well as to the weekly posters in the teachers' room. Both the monthly calendars and weekly posters will reflect the addition of the new activities to the activities attempted the previous year.

As the new learning activities are being tried in the various sectors of the school community, the project director will set up meetings with the student advisory committee, and schedule meetings for the various clusters of teachers to review their progress every four to six weeks. In other words, the same feedback and communication systems of the previous year will be initiated.

The home committee will continue to send out the monthly suggestions for home learning activities that complement those taking place in the school. These suggestions will take into account the addition of the second year's activities to the activities initiated in the previous year. Since the children will have moved up to a new grade, many of the activities for that student will be new that year. Parents will continue to be canvassed on a random basis for their perceptions and suggestions concerning the ethical education of their children.

End-of-semester assessments and parent surveys will again be administered and their results studied by teachers, staff and steering committee. By now the information should begin to take on a relatively stable pattern, and the steering committee may want to make some new recommendations concerning those problem areas which keep surfacing in these assessments and surveys.

The Second Year of Implementation, Second Semester

The second semester begins with the faculty and staff studying the end-of-semester report of the steering committee on the results of the parent survey, the student assessment, and the teacher review sessions. There may be some adjustments needed in their planned learning activities for the second semester in the light of the results of the survey and assessment. In any event, the project director continues to put out the monthly calendars and the weekly posters and to schedule the feedback sessions with the students and the review sessions with the faculty. The home committee continues to send out suggestions for parents and to seek feedback via their telephone spot checks with parents.

The steering committee convenes the working committees and subcommittees for the design of the final plans for phase three of the implementation. The committees put together their new set of ethical learning activities and the steering committee coordinates all four sets of plans into a preliminary master plan. This will constitute the agenda for the final summer workshops when the whole faculty and staff will finish the fuller design and assessment of the learning activities.

With the completion of the semester's initiatives in the new learning activities, the parent surveys and student assessment at the end of the semester are once again administered. The parent surveys should include additional questions about the perceived helpfulness of continuing the suggestions for home activities and the use of the surveys to garner parental sentiments. There should be additional space for parents to suggest improvements in the way the school works with them. In other words, the school wants to know whether the parents think the school should continue the intense involvement of the parents in home-based learning activities, and whether it should continue to promote the intense communication with and feedback from the parents. One would expect by now that the parents have come to see the value of their involvement in their children's education, and would want to recommend that it continue. However, there may be specific 'glitches' or shortcomings in the system which could be brought to light by such an inquiry.

Again, the end of the school year should be the occasion for a big party or picnic in which the parents, teachers and students celebrate the work of the year. Appropriate awards should also be given out at this time. Perhaps the school board should be involved in sponsoring this celebration and providing visible evidence of its appreciation of the extra efforts of the parents and staff.

The Third Year of Implementation

The Summer Workshops

The steering committee will have gathered the evaluation information from the teachers, the parents and the students, sifted through it, and once again come out with a summary report and recommendations. This will constitute the initial agenda for discussions by the faculty, staff and parents. They should look for problems in the connecting of ethical lessons across academic disciplines and across the other three areas, and seek to strengthen those connections. The ethical lesson is more likely to be learned more thoroughly when it is recognized as occurring under a variety of circumstances. They should also check to see whether the learnings brought about by the second-year activities were qualitatively enhanced because of the experience with the first-year activities. Logically, one would expect that to happen. By studying these connections and relationships, the faculty, staff and parents might get a better understanding of how to proceed in their work of filling out the learning activities for the third year of implementation.

As they take up their design tasks for phase three, the teachers and parents should be looking ahead to building into their plans ways to *institutionalize* the learnings they are designing. That is, they should seek to ensure that this school-wide effort at ethical education becomes permanent, becomes part of the life blood of the school community. This means that it has all the organizational support it needs, support such as its costs being included in the regular yearly budget; adequate administrative support; adequate policy support by the board so that new teachers are expected to participate in these ethical learning activities; the clear expectation by the board that parents will participate fully in the effort. In other words, the experiment in building an ethical school would seem at this point to have been successful and can be thought of as no longer an experiment but as a legitimate part of the goals and purposes of the school. Hence, it should receive the same kind of institutional support as any other essential ingredient of the school, such as the science or language arts program. Even though this effort has not cost the school the addition of a new department of two or three teachers, there is danger that in times of fiscal austerity, the latest program costs are often the first to be cut. The idea is to ensure that this does not happen. The school administration may want, therefore, in this summer, to institute a requirement for all new teachers at the school to undergo an intensive orientation to the ethical education they are expected to espouse as a member of the teaching staff. They may also want to consider whether the work of the project director will be carried on after the third year by someone in the administration, or by a lead teacher, or under some other rubric.

The Third Year of Implementation, First Semester

After the opening meeting conducted by the steering committee to lay out the master plan for the year, the faculty sets to work on the complete set of learning activities in their respective areas. That is to say, to the learning activities of year one and year two of the implementation they now add the new learning activities. The new activities should enlarge and deepen the learnings of the first two years. This will be an opportunity for teachers to develop a full rationale that connects all their ethical learning activities together. Besides reflecting on what works or not, teachers should be asked to reflect on the connections they see between all the ethical learning activities in their areas. These reflections will make up the agenda of their discussion every four to six weeks. Besides scheduling these activities, the project director will also make available the monthly calendars and the weekly posters in the teachers' room.

Parents will also hold one or more meetings with the steering committee to review the master plan for the year and the procedures the home committee will be following with them. They will be asked to spend more time helping their children make the connections with all the school's learning activities and the home activities. By now, the students will have built up a considerable history of experiences with ethical learnings, and parents will be asked to initiate conversations with their children which might generate insight into the connections between present and past learnings. The monthly suggestions of the home committee might supply examples of some of these relationships, so parents would have some illustrative material with which to work.

As in the past, the results of teachers' reflections on the new learning activities, reports from the student advisory committee, end-of-semester student assessments, and parents' surveys will be weighed by the steering committee, which will issue a report and recommendations at the beginning of the second semester.

The Third Year of Implementation, Second Semester

The process will continue as it has in previous semesters, with the project director and the home committees engaged in the various monitoring activities as in the past. The steering committee, however, will not have to call the various working committees and subcommittees together for further design work. The steering committee will have a major task, however, that is to engage in a thorough evaluation of the implementation phase.

The Evaluation

I would suggest that the school board engage an outside consultant to bring in a team of evaluators to conduct a formal evaluation of the project. Although the formal evaluation would be conducted in the second semester of this third year of implementation, the evaluation team might have been called together earlier, so that they would have had time to gain a sense of the purposes and scope of the project, as well as to meet some of the major players in the project. This evaluation team would be supplied with all the reports of the steering committee since its first meeting. It would meet with the student advisory committee and with the home committee to review their impressions of the implementation. The team would visit classes and other activities around the school to get a first-hand look at some of the learning activities. Extensive interviews with teachers should probe their level of commitment and understanding of their part in the project. The evaluation team may want to devise its own survey instruments for gathering information from the parents, students and teachers concerning the impact of the project.

One of the standard strategies in conducting an evaluation of this type is to conduct a pre-test and a post-test to see what progress students have made. When one is talking about basic learnings in mathematics or language usage, such pre and post-test evaluations are somewhat useful, because the technology of constructing such tests is relatively well developed, and there is a substantial accumulation of national and regional data which allows testers to develop national and regional norms for various age groups. Hence test scores of children before the new program will indicate where they stood relative to national and regional samples of youngsters of similar age and background, and where they stood in relation to those samples after the program. If they showed a larger than expected advance over the regional and national samples, then evaluators conclude that some of that advance was due to the strength or quality of the new program.

In this instance, however, I doubt that such strategies would be workable. First of all, we are talking about a process which allows the school community to decide which ethical qualities and values it wants to promote. There may not be tests which measure the unique constellation of ethical values which the school community has chosen. Furthermore, there are not tests of sufficient sophistication available with a history of usage on a national or regional basis which might provide us with some comparisons. Because the learning activities are being developed within the school, rather than by a test constructor, there is no warrant for supposing that tests constructed by someone outside of that school community would be testing the learning that was intended in the construction of those learning activities.

Although it might not pass the test for scientific proof, surveys which asked parents and teachers whether they could observe growth in the youngsters as a result of the school's efforts, growth which they had not observed before the program was initiated, may provide some legitimate sense of whether the program was moving in the right direction. Some kind of long range follow-up might be devised, whereby parents and students would be surveyed every four or five years after graduation to get a sense of the lasting impact of the school's efforts.

Comparisons with other, similar student populations could also be devised based on gross measures such as the comparative incidents of school violence, theft, truancy, student–teacher conflict, etc. These kinds of evaluative studies can become quite expensive and would require mounting a considerable research effort. Most schools will be content with a more modest evaluation. State departments of education, however, might be interested in supporting a more ambitious form of evaluative research, were there to be a state-wide effort to build ethical schools.

In any event, the formal evaluation should be completed by the end of the school year so that the whole school community can study the concluding report of findings and recommendations. The evaluation may reveal an overall satisfaction with the project, but also reveal two or three consistent problems which need attending to. This then becomes the ongoing agenda of the school for the succeeding years. The school board should request a similar evaluation every four or five years. Now that the school has a baseline of information from which to work, subsequent evaluations may be able to make comparisons and contrasts with earlier findings.

The Conclusion of the 'Project': The Beginning of the Ethical School

At this point, the school should move beyond referring to its efforts at ethical education as 'the project'. It should consider that it is now a natural part of school life. As a way of signaling this transition, some appropriate transitional ceremony or celebration should be held. This ceremony should include some formal statement by the school board and by the school administration that indicates that ethical education is now considered an essential ingredient of the education of all youngsters at this school. That formal statement should include specific institutional supports for such a vital ingredient, supports that touch upon the school's regular curriculum, library and media supports, administrative support, permanent parental arrangements with the school, contractual agreements between teachers and the board, etc. The school should build in appropriate rituals and ceremonies on an annual basis which accentuate the ethical character of the education which takes place at the school. Graduation criteria should explicitly mention this feature of the school. This essential ingredient should be embodied in stories and traditions, such that incoming students breathe in the spirit behind the school's practice.

It would be a mistake to think that once the project was completed the school had achieved a perfect, or even a good program in ethical education. Just as the science curriculum undergoes changes and modifications, just as citizenship education develops over the years, so too, the staff will grow in its understanding and ability to improve its programs. New learning activities will be devised and old ones discarded. That is the nature of development in schools. In a sense the building of an ethical school never ceases, just as the building of a democracy is never completed. What the process described in the past several chapters will have achieved, with luck and fortitude, is a solid beginning, but only a beginning. Once the parents and teachers get used to ethical education as being a mainstream concern of the community, they will continue to devise ways to improve it — or they should. An ethical school that keeps teaching the same exact lessons for three or four years in a row is on its way to ritualizing ethical education, that is, on its way to losing touch with the realities of people's lives, which continually throw up new ethical questions and challenges. But this challenge of continuous regeneration is a challenge that faces schools on all fronts.

Chapter 9

Reality Versus the Plan

Anyone familiar with the day-to-day events in classrooms and school buildings knows that the neat logic of the planning process outlined in the previous chapters runs counter to the messy and unpredictable realities of teaching and administering a school. The design phase and the implementation phase presented earlier is the work of a designer, a planner, a curriculum developer, an administrator. Things are laid out in proper sequence, according to a reasonable projection of how a local school community might pull off such a venture. It is helpful to see the project described in its entirety so one has a sense of a beginning, a middle and a successful completion. It is not helpful to create the illusion that things will in fact work out this way. Any group of educators who wants to build an ethical school should know that the process will not be as neat and orderly as the process described in the previous chapters. The process will be probably be contested, misunderstood, distorted, mismanaged and resisted by many, as well as embraced enthusiastically by some. Hence, it may be salutary to reflect on the realities of schools which will make the building of an ethical school difficult — not impossible, but just plain difficult. These realities are the students, the teachers, the institution and the nature of ethical life itself.

The Plan Versus the Realities of Students

Whether working with a class of twenty to thirty students in elementary, middle or high school classes, teaching anything is difficult. Every person in that class has a unique combination of talents, shortcomings, personal history, social class background, aspirations, impulses, handicaps, emotions, and prior experiences with teachers and schools. At any given moment in the school day, a student can be up or down, focused or dreamy, tired or energetic, interested or bored. Those dispositions affect the ability of a teacher to connect with that student at any given moment in the day, or on any given day of the week. Curriculum planners often seem to assume that all twenty or thirty children are continuously attentive in class, responsive to the teacher's directives, motivated to want to learn any particular lesson. Some commentators believe that 'effective' teachers should be able to control the classroom to such an extent that they keep all of the students continuously focused on the learning tasks throughout the class.

The reality of classrooms is quite different. Children are perpetually squirming, scratching, distracted, fidgety. Most of them don't want to be there. They would much prefer being out on the playground, or anywhere else but the classroom, with their friends. Most of them are not interested in studying history, or geography or science or mathematics. Furthermore, since they are forced to be in school, many of them find ways of resisting the control which the adult community imposes on them, either by fooling around, getting the teacher off track, passing notes to their friends, or, at the very least, figuring out how not to get called on in class. Teachers who bear down too hard on students, who do not communicate care and respect for them, but on the contrary ridicule and humiliate them do not get the students' best efforts, but rather minimal compliance. Often students will figure out a way to make those teachers' lives miserable as well. Good teachers know how to mix control and care; they know that the students' cooperation is not automatic, that it must be solicited and earned through the quality of relationships they establish, and the agreements and compromises they strike with them.

Depending on the background of the students, especially the home background, some will be more amenable, some less, to the kind of ethical learning the teacher is proposing. Whether the school is in the inner city or in the affluent suburbs, there is no 'better' environment to grow up in. Children of affluence sometimes have more emotionally crippling home environments than children of poverty. Teachers have to work with the students they get, and what they get is usually a mixed bag with a wide variety of backgrounds and needs. Hence teachers may find that a learning activity dealing with an ethical issue will appeal to some students but not to others. In some cases the students may resist the intended lesson and come up with another viewpoint that the teacher hadn't thought about, but which has a certain legitimacy. Being open to such turns of events often takes the lesson down unexplored tracks, sometimes ending up in insight, sometimes trailing off into confusion. Good teachers live with such uncertainty.[1]

The diversity of students' cultural, racial, ethnic, class and family backgrounds make the evaluation of expressions of ethical behavior difficult. One cannot expect all students to behave in some officially predetermined ethical way. One has to expect a diversity of responses to the ethical curriculum, and try to understand the motivation and reasoning behind it. This does not mean that teachers cannot attempt to deal with common ethical values in their learning activities; it means, rather, that there will be a plurality of responses, all, or most of which may be entirely legitimate expressions of that common ethical value.

The Plan Versus the Reality of Teachers

There are two views of teaching. One is that teaching should involve relatively uniform behaviors which research has shown to be effective in producing student learning. Whether it be the Hunter method, the classroom effectiveness method, or some other set of competencies, good teaching, so it is assumed in this perspective, should be distinguishable from bad teaching, the one producing results and the other not producing results. Within this viewpoint, it is possible to have 'teacher-proof' curriculum materials and lesson plans; that is, no matter who is teaching the course, if they simply follow the outline of the lesson contained in the teachers' manual, the learning is bound to occur.[2]

The other view of teaching sees it as a much more uncertain craft, embedded in contexts and situational variables over which teachers often have little control. Leiberman and Miller say it well.

> No uncertainty is greater than the one that surrounds the connection between teaching and learning. A teacher does his or her best, develops curricula, tries new approaches, works with individuals and groups, and yet never knows for sure what are the effects. One hopes the children will get it, but one is never sure. A teacher operates out of a kind of blind faith that with enough in the way of planning, rational schemes, objectives and learning activities some learning will take place. But a teacher also knows that some learnings happen that are significant and never planned for and that other learnings never take hold, despite the best of professional intentions.[3]

While it is possible to argue that teaching is not necessarily one or the other, that it is possible to hold that certain teaching practices are preferable to others (being patient rather than being overbearing; using psychological persuasion rather than physical force), I tend to follow the thinking and research of many scholars that the personality of the teacher matters very much in what gets taught and learned. This view tends to see teaching as requiring connections between the unique personality of the teacher and the unique personalities of the students. That being the case, any curriculum or syllabus will be taught differently and learned differently because of the differences in teachers' and in students' personalities.

More than a little insight into varieties of personalities is provided by the theory of personality types, developed by Isabel Myers, which in turn is based on earlier theories of Carl Jung.[4] From the perspective of this theory, we can find teachers who are extroverted (get energy and insight from interacting with people), and others who are introverted (tend to think things over by themselves and take experiences inside); teachers who enjoy taking things apart and putting them together (love breaking things down into small details, working with pieces of things) and others who instinctively move toward the larger synthetic view of wholes (are inclined toward intuitive insight into relationships and a gestalt of the larger landscape); teachers who are comfortable with thinking things through (who follow a logical train of thought, who conceptualize and talk in conceptual frameworks), and others who more spontaneously feel their way into a topic (who come to knowledge by tasting it, letting it settle in the viscera, who probe with images and metaphors and respond with comfort or discomfort to experience); teachers who instinctively want to round things out, to define them, to bring them to completion (who come quickly to conclusions and judgments, and are uncomfortable with loose ends), and others who are quite content to keep looking, who let things trail off into indefiniteness (who believe that truth is never exhausted, but encompasses still more of the unexplored and unexpressed).

These various personality traits combine differently in different teachers, so that in one classroom one might find a teacher who is introverted, likes to fiddle with small details, likes to line things up logically and explore their theoretical implications, and comes quickly to judgments about things, while in the next classroom, one might find a teacher who is extroverted, intuitively leaps to insights, feels knowledge rather than thinks about the logical explanation of it, and simply enjoys the perpetual exploration of the terrain without having to achieve closure. Were they both teaching a Shakespearean play, students would experience the play differently, even though, on a test, they might all know the names of the main characters. Were these two teachers probing the ethics of local zoning regulations and public housing patterns, again, students would be led to approach the ethical issues differently, even though they might know similar facts about the topic, and come to the same ethical conclusions. Of course, the picture becomes even more complex when we realize that not only do teachers express this great diversity of personality types, but the twenty or thirty students in the class reflect similar diversity.

Besides personality types, teachers also differ in their educational platforms.[5] Educational platform is a metaphor taken from politics, where political parties have a set of principles and propositions on issues which make up the 'platform' on which they take a political stand for what they believe in, and which expresses what they promise the voters. Teachers' educational platforms express the normative assumptions, principles, beliefs and values that guide their teaching activity. Seldom are these stated explicitly, but they are nonetheless highly influential in their teaching. When asked to make their platform explicit, teachers will state their platforms in a variety of formats, often by stories, sometimes in brief, apodictic statements. However they are expressed, platforms usually encompass the following elements: the aims of education; the teacher's preferred pedagogy; the image of the learner; the social significance of the students' learning; the image of the curriculum; the image of the teacher; the most important things students should learn.[6] One might find platforms of great variety amidst the teachers in any given school. Clearly, where a teacher stands on various elements of the platform will tend to influence what gets taught and how it gets taught.

Beyond the platform are other sources of diversity among the teaching faculty. In many schools there are clear differences in perceived political influence within the school. Some people are perceived as having the principal's ear, or as having connections with the superintendent. Some people are resentfully perceived as always wanting to be in charge of whatever new project happens to be hot that year. In other cases, changes cause resentment because of perceptions of lessened political influence within the school; those who used to be close to the center of influence are now edged to the periphery by newcomers. All of these perceptions, whether based in fact or imagination, lead people to oppose, reject, scuttle, or contest all attempts to do something new. In a process such as building an ethical school, these perceptions may lead some people eventually to give verbal assent, but to offer minimal compliance with the implementation plans.

In any given high school, one academic department may work very closely together, enjoy strong leadership, and have a history of being acknowledged as the strongest department in the school, while another department may be made up of very contentious individuals who cannot work well together, and whose leadership is weak.[7] The strong department will work well together in generating relatively similar, high quality learning activities in the ethical curriculum, whereas the fragmented department may exhibit a rather random and sporadic effort at participating in the planning and the implementation of the ethical curriculum.

Besides the reality of fluctuating moods and energies that result in some teachers being up on a given day, while others are down, there are seasonal ebbs and flow of energy and enthusiasm. Late winter is hardly the most enthusiastic time around schools, whereas the first month of most semesters is a time of optimism and high energy. Hence variations of interest and enthusiasm for ethical learning activities will be influenced by the calendar.

One of the most serious causes of teacher variations in response to the planning and implementation process is a cultural mindlessness and insensitivity about ethical issues which affects many to some degree or other. As Maxine Greene put it,

> It is far too easy for teachers, like other people, to play their roles and do their jobs without serious consideration of the good and the right . . . If teachers today are to initiate young people into an ethical existence, they themselves must attend more fully than they normally have to their own lives and its requirements; they have to break with the mechanical life, to overcome their own submergence in the habitual, even in what they conceive to be the virtuous, and ask the 'why' with which learning and moral reasoning begin.[8]

If teachers are to influence students to live as authentic persons who act out of a sense of autonomy, connectedness and transcendence, as persons concerned about justice in their personal and social lives, genuinely caring for other people, and courageous enough to critique the ingrained practices within society which oppress others, then teachers will have to present themselves to students as people who strive to live their own lives this way. This will require many teachers to take the ethical challenges in their lives much more seriously than they do at present. Where students experience this variability among their teachers, they will no doubt experience differently the lessons those teachers teach as well.

When one stirs all these variables among the teaching faculty into the soup of school life, it is not difficult to imagine how the logical and orderly progression of a planning or implementation process can become contentious, uncertain, disorderly, disjointed and difficult to sustain.

The Plan Versus the Reality of Institutional Life

By the institutional life of the school I mean all those regularities of day-to-day practice which, through the weight of their repetition, come tacitly to define reality. These regularities become 'the way things are around here', or 'the way things are done around here'. No one questions them; to do so would convey a reckless irreverence, a shocking lack of sensitivity to convention. Often these regularities come to define part of the culture of the institution.

One aspect of the culture of schools is the culture of teacher isolation.[9] Teachers spend most of their day in school working behind classroom doors with their students, separated from other teachers who are working with their own students. Although they might see one another in the teachers' room during the day, they rarely, if ever, speak about what they are doing in their classrooms. They might speak about a difficult student, or a pesky parent, but they rarely ask another teacher's opinion about a particular teaching strategy they may be trying for the first time. Because there is the belief that teaching is an art, that the links between teaching and learning are uncertain, that the scientific knowledge base for teaching is weak, because the goals of teaching are vague and conflicting, and the professional support for the beginning learning of the craft is so weak — for all these reasons, teachers are socialized into a privatization of their teaching. As long as the children are not tearing the place to pieces, and there is some evidence that they are learning, what a teacher does in his or her classroom appears to be of no concern to anyone else in the school.

Because of this culture of isolation and privatization, teachers rarely, if ever, discuss their teaching. Hence the process of discussion and generation of ideas for building an ethical school will go against the grain of most school cultures. Initially, teachers may complain about wasting time in these discussions; it may simply be inconceivable to them that they might collaborate in putting together a curriculum, and beyond that, that they might discuss the results of their common attempts to teach ethical lessons. Their institutional reality has simply precluded that possibility. To suggest that teachers change that cultural practice might seem to some teachers a bold affront to their independence.

Another part of the culture of schools is the culture of passivity (which is reinforced by the culture of isolation). Teachers are accustomed to administrators making the institutional decisions. Administrators make up the master schedule and simply notify the teachers of what schedule and which students have been assigned to them. Teachers are told of new student regulations which they are expected to enforce. New calendars for the school year are routinely passed by the school board and the administrative staff without anyone thinking to consult the teachers, unless an assertive teachers' association demands it. In many systems, textbooks are chosen by central office supervisors, or even by administrators at the regional or state levels. Walls are knocked down, hallways carpeted, new ceilings put in, rooms painted — all by administrative decisions. Teachers simply go along with all these institutional decisions. Hence, when it comes to engaging teachers in the discussions about and designs of an ethical school, administrators may wonder at the apathetic response from the teachers. Teachers have been conditioned that, when it comes to school-wide decisions and policies, their opinions are not considered of much value: 'What is all this fuss about *now*? The administrators want an ethical school, let them bring in the experts and tell us what to do.' It is hard for teachers to believe that administrators want them to become actively engaged in building an ethical school, when they have never been asked to be engaged like this before. It will take some convincing.

The institutional forms of using space, time and personnel come eventually to define not only 'the way things are done around here', but the way things *should* be done around here. Institutional forms like schedules, departments, classroom size, length of class periods, length of class days, length of school years, grading systems, discipline systems, promotion criteria, graduation requirements, guidance systems, teacher professional days, even the availability of bathrooms shape the activity of students and teachers into patterns that become, paradoxically, *comfortable*. For some, these forms come to be preferred. Everyone in the school has made accommodations to them, worked out ways of surviving despite them, found ways to get around them when necessary, used them in one way or another to gain some advantage (students can fake their work just long enough to avoid detection within the standard class period; teachers can improvise a lesson just long enough during a standard class period to avoid the students' perception that they were unprepared).

The routine after a while becomes a narcotic, preventing anything really significant from happening because there isn't enough time or space or money ever available at any one time to get beyond the routines into something deeper or more adventuresome. After a while, everyone in the institution has been socialized into the conspiracy by which doing little, even in honors classes, becomes the norm. Hence, to ask teachers to take themselves seriously and to construct learning activities that might require different institutional arrangements of curriculum boundaries, class schedules, promotion criteria, and the like, when this has never before happened in their professional experience, is asking a lot.

Within the institutional formats, administrators have become distanced from the essential work of schools, namely teaching and learning. Administrators formulate and enact institutional policies such as dress codes, graduation requirements, rules governing traffic into and out of the cafeteria and up and down stairwells, health and safety regulations in gym classes and locker rooms — regulations which all students and teachers are to observe uniformly. These policies tend to focus on institutional control of student actions. Many of these policies and rules appear to expect student misbehavior, stupidity or mischievousness, to anticipate it, judge it and prevent it. Yet most administrators do not know most of the students in their schools in the way teachers know them. Administrators are used to administering institutional things such as budgets, bus schedules, fire drills, assembly schedules, parent–teacher nights, schedules of interscholastic events, and the like. To ask them to become involved in the ethical education of students, where they would have to intuitively understand the students well enough to know what it is in institutional life which students find alienating is asking a lot. Likewise, to ask administrators who are not intimately involved in daily learning tasks with students to reorganize their thinking so that they can participate genuinely in the conversations about possible learning activities for students that would contribute to building an ethical school is asking a lot.

The Plan Versus the Complexity of Ethical Choice

Besides the aforementioned obstacles to the logical and orderly planning and implementing of ethical education, there is the complexity and ambiguity of much of ethical experience itself. Sometimes ethical choices are simple and straightforward. Should I walk out of the store without paying for the merchandise? Should I falsely accuse someone of breaking the window, when I am the one who broke it? Usually, the answers these ethical questions pose no problems. But other situations may not be so clear. If I were to put myself in a student's place, I would have to struggle with many of their questions. How should I treat a bully who is picking on my little brother? How should I respond to the demands of a drunken parent? How should I respond to a police officer who uses an ethnic slur when addressing me? How do I respond to my best friend who wants to copy my homework? How do I respond when my classmates are scapegoating a student I don't like? How do I respond to a reckless driver who pulls out of a side street just in front of me, without even slowing down at the stop sign? How do I respond to another person who shoves me against the lockers in the school corridor? How do I respond when I see some of my friends making fun of a handicapped person? For many young people, the complexities of social life — when their own identities are only in the process of being formed, and their loyalties uncertain — leave them morally conflicted or uncertain. Not a few adults face similar uncertainties.

It is relatively easy to speak in generalities of autonomy, connectedness and transcendence, as well as justice, caring and critique. In lived experience, however, circumstances often pose two or three apparently valid interpretations of what comprises autonomy, connectedness and transcendence. In other circumstances, our connectedness may be to two people to whom we owe allegiance, but only one of whom can be served by our decision, while the other is harmed by our decision.

In any given ethical decision we often find layers of motives, some of which are self-serving, some of which are more altruistic. Most situations in our lives involve ambiguities, ironies and paradoxes. We are seldom all aligned in one direction toward virtue. Self-deception and rationalization constantly intrude, often at a subliminal level that avoids detection until someone else points it out to us. For persons of integrity, living ethically usually involves struggle and conflict; even the virtuous have their moments of weariness and discouragement, when the easy way out is chosen over the more ethically 'correct' response.

Building an ethical school will demand that teachers always communicate that they care about the moral tone of the school community. That caring, however, will always have to be mixed with sensitivity to the difficulty that even mature adults, let alone children and adolescents, have with consistently living an ethical life. Teachers will have to set limits, but the limits should be imposed with love and compassion. The ethical school will exhibit 'tough love' at times; at other times it will exhibit unconditional love; it should teach students how to forgive themselves and each other; it should also acknowledge that ethical values are expressed in a variety of ways, and be aware that sometimes students will express their values in unpredictable and unconventional ways. The ethical school will stand for ethical values; it will also avoid the self-righteousness of the ethical know-it-all, admitting that in some instances certainty eludes us all.

For the ethical school to succeed, all the members will need constantly to remind themselves that this is a human enterprise. As such, they should expect mistakes and imperfections. They will have to remind themselves that human beings are flawed and inconsistent, that despite their best intentions, ego will creep in to even the most altruistic of enterprises. The effort has to be entered upon with a sense of humility and sustained with a sense of compassion; otherwise it will defeat itself by expecting too much and by becoming a prisoner of its unrealistic expectations. The community will have to remind itself constantly that one learns to become ethical perhaps more often by learning from failures than by celebrating successes.

Summary

At the beginning of this book, I rehearsed various standard objections claiming to show why the attempt to build an ethical school was doomed to failure. I then countered those objections with persuasive arguments. Now, in this last chapter, am I allowing myself to be defeated by new doubts? To think so would be a misreading of the argument of this chapter.

I believe that educators must make the effort to build an ethical school. Ethical education is integral to any process which deserves the name of education, for knowledge that is important to the human family has, in one way or another, ethical implications. In our exploration of a rationale and a process for building an ethical school it is natural that high expectations would arise. Without backing down from those high expectations, it is important to realize that the experience of the ethical community will always involve the comedy and tragedy of the human situation. Ethical education is not a simple training in the predisposition to be ethical, the lessons of which, once learned, guarantee an ethical adulthood. Ethical education is a lifelong education. It takes place simultaneously with our efforts to be human. We learn to be human in the *struggle* for integrity. Virtue is not something we achieve and then continue to possess. We continue to be capable of doing evil. Virtue is always out in front of us to be achieved; it involves a perpetual doing. The human person is always incomplete. In a sense we do not create ourselves, we do ourselves. We do not make 'good works'; we do good. We can't lay it out ahead of time. We can't say, now that I have developed and possess this virtue, I know how to act in this or that circumstance, in advance. The virtuous act must be continuously sought.[10] Since ethical education is a lifelong experience, it should begin in school so that the process of ethical learning can become more intentionally reflected upon and its lessons more clearly learned.

Paradoxically, we learn what it is to be human as well when we *fail* as when we succeed. In failure, we learn the hard lesson of our limits and the ambivalence of our motives, and the wonderful lesson of being forgiven by our fellows. We learn through failure the lesson of compassion, compassion for ourselves and compassion for our brothers and sisters. We discover the emptiness of a self-centered life, and the richness of a life whose connections sustain us even in our failures. In the pursuit and occasional achievement of some virtuous activity, we discover the quiet joy of enhancing someone else's life, the satisfaction of easing someone else's pain, the surprising pleasure when our honoring a relationship is acknowledged, the paradoxical fulfillment of ourselves when we give away ourselves. The learning is in the striving, not simply of the individual but in experiencing the striving of the community, where we gain our humanity in interaction with other humans who are struggling with all the heroic ambiguities of the human condition. A perfect ethical community would probably bore us to tears; we would not recognize it as a human community. A human community is a community that expresses the full range of the journey toward its fulfillment, in short a divine comedy. In school, we learn that our life, collectively and individually, is a divine comedy, but that the direction it takes is our responsibility.

Building an ethical school, then, calls for great courage, a modicum of intelligence, lots of humility, humor and compassion, and an unyielding hope in the endurance and heroism of human beings. It is a dream worthy of educators.

Notes

1 See Joseph McDonald's (1992) wonderfully insightful book, *Teaching: Making Sense of an Uncertain Craft*, New York, Teachers College Press.
2 Eleanor Duckworth's (1987) delightful book, '*The Having of Wonderful Ideas' and Other Essays on Teaching and Learning*, New York, Teachers College Press, offers very detailed arguments why this perspective on teaching is so misguided.

3 Lieberman, A. and Miller, L. (1984) *Teachers, Their World and Their Work: Implications for School Improvement*, Alexandria, VA, Association for Supervision and Curriculum Development, pp. 2–3.

4 Meyers, I. (1962) *Manual: The Myers-Briggs Type Indicator*, Palo Alto, CA, Consulting Psychologists Press.

5 Sergiovanni, T.J. and Starratt, R.J. (1993) *Supervision: A Redefinition*, New York, McGraw-Hill, pp. 133–45.

6 Sergiovanni and Starratt (1993) pp. 140–1.

7 See Susan Moore Johnson's (1990) research on academic departments in 'The primacy and potential of high school departments', in McLaughlin, M.W., Talbert, J.E. and Bascia, N. (Eds) *The Contexts of Teaching in Secondary Schools: Teachers' Realities*, New York, Teachers College Press.

8 Greene, M. (1978) *Landscapes of Learning*, New York, Teachers College Press, p. 46.

9 See Leiberman and Miller (1984) pp. 1–15, for a sympathetic treatment of the isolation of teachers.

10 I have been helped to grasp this insight by Gilbert C. Meilaender (1984) in his *The Theory and Practice of Virtue*, Notre Dame, IN, University of Notre Dame Press.

Selected Resources in Ethical Education

What follows is a list of organizations and places where resources and information on various aspects of ethical education may be located. Information about the majority of these resources has been culled from Thomas Lickona's (1991) study, *Educating Character* (New York, Bantam Books), which is itself an excellent resource. These are not the only groups producing materials, but they seem to be groups that have had several years of experience refining learning activities that seem to work for large numbers of children and their parents. Many of these groups will be networked with other groups, some of whom are developing additional resources. When writing to these groups, be sure to ask them for information on other groups which are developing materials.

1 The Child Development Project of San Ramon, California, promotes a five-pronged program: 1) cooperative learning; 2) using children's literature to develop empathy and understanding of others; 3) exposure to prosocial models or examples; 4) involvement in cross-age helping relationships; 5) developmental discipline. Other school districts have used their materials and, according to Lickona, are highly enthusiastic about them. Those seeking information on cross-age tutoring, family homework assignments, and a design for creating a caring school community should write to The Child Development Project, 111 Deerwood Place, Suite 165, San Ramon, CA 94583; telephone: 415–838–7633.

2 Effective Parenting Information Center (EPIC) provides parenting workshops, coupled with a classroom curriculum,

Growing Up Together. Write EPIC, State University of New York at Buffalo, 1300 Elmwood Ave, Buffalo, NY 14222; telephone: 716–884–4064.

3   The publication *Family Guides* informs parents of value lessons taught in their child's classroom that day and suggests how to follow up at home. For information on this publication and on another resource on intergenerational programs, *The Connection Dimension*, write to Scotia-Glenville Central Schools, Scotia, New York 12302.

4   For information on how to participate in community action projects, write to Choosing to Participate, Facing History and Ourselves, 25 Kennard Road, Brookline, MA 02146; telephone: 617–232–1595.

5   For how-to manuals on community service projects, write to Winnie Pardo, Shoreham-Wading River Middle School, Randall Road, Shoreham, NY 11786. See also *Wingspread: Principles of Good Practice for Combining Service and Learning*, The Johnson Foundation, Inc., Racine, WI 53401.

6   The Giraffe Project is interested in 'ordinary' heroes, people who act courageously and with compassion, but who seldom get the headlines. They have teachers' kits and materials to develop a Giraffe Project at your school. Write to The Giraffe Project, 120 Second Street, PO Box 759, Langly, Whidbey Island, WA 98260; telephone: 1–800–344–8255.

7   Amnesty International has a *Children's Urgent Action* newsletter each month, in which it provides information about other children in danger or in detention as prisoners of conscience. For information about how to set up an Amnesty International Chapter for children or older students, write to Amnesty International/USA, 322 Eighty Avenue, New York, NY 10001; telephone: 212–807–8400.

8   On issues of worldwide hunger, disease and poverty see Oxfam's newsletter and other information. Write to Oxfam America, 115 Broadway, Boston, MA 02116; telephone: 617–482–1211.

9   Conflict-resolution materials for teaching youngsters how to resolve their conflicts peacefully are available from Children's Creative Response to Conflict Program, Fellowship of Reconciliation, Box 271, 523 North Broadway, Nyack, NY 10960–0271; telephone: 914–358–4601. For another resource, *The Directory of School Mediation and Conflict Resolution Programs*, write to the National Association for Mediation in Education

(NAME), 425 Amity Street, Amherst, MA 01002; telephone: 413–545–2462.

10 For computer software on teaching decision-making skills on moral issues, drugs, sex, friendship, conflicts, truth-telling, etc., contact Tom Snyder Productions, 90 Sherman Street, Cambridge, MA 02140–9923; telephone: 1–800–342–0236.

11 The Commission for Research and Development of the Jesuit Secondary Education Association has developed a comprehensive curriculum framework that includes learning activities dealing with friendship, family and social justice. For information about The Curriculum Improvement Process, write to The Commission on Research and Development, Jesuit Secondary Association, Fordham University At Lincoln Center, New York, NY 10023.

12 For curriculum materials on social responsibility contact Education for Social Responsibility, 23 Garden Street, Cambridge, MA 02138; telephone: 617–492–1764.

13 For an overview of some ethical education programs in the schools, see the January 1991 special issue of *Ethics*, a publication of the Josephson Institute of Ethics, 310 Washington Boulevard, Suite 104, Marina del Rey, CA 90292; telephone: 213–306–1868.

14 The Hamilton, Ontario, Board of Education has prepared a citizenship program called *Prepare* for youngsters in grades four to six. For teens they developed *Preparing Adolescents for Tomorrow*. For information contact Values Education Consultant, Board of Education for the City of Hamilton, PO Box 558, 100 Main Street West, Hamilton, Ontario L8N 3L1, Canada; telephone: 416–527–5092.

15 Professor Thomas L. Dynneson, School of Education at the University of Texas in Odessa, Texas, has published several reports on citizenship education through the Citizen Education Development Study Project, a project at the Center for Educational Research at Stanford (CERAS), Stanford University, Stanford, CA.

Annotated Bibliography

This appendix contains descriptions of books that helped shape or confirm ideas contained in this book. It is not a complete annotated bibliography of all the possible books on the topic of ethics and ethical/moral education. It is offered as a help to those who would want to expand their understanding of the various schools of thought touched upon here. At the early stages of exploratory discussions about the possibility of building an ethical school and running throughout the initiation discussions of the foundational characteristics and ethical frameworks, I would expect teachers to be looking for some reading material. I would hope that other helpful books, not mentioned here, would be discovered along the way. Presented in alphabetical order, the bibliography does not list, for instance, the five most important books; rather, the description of a book should suggest its value to the potential reader.

AIKEN, W.M. (1942) *The Story of the Eight-Year Study*, New York, Harper and Row.
Aiken describes the most ambitious effort to transform secondary schools in the United States. The effort embraced democracy as the purposeful mission of schooling, and proposed that secondary schools would demonstrate, *in all phases of their activity*, the kind of life in which we as citizens of a democratic society believe. The book demonstrates, in a rich variety of approaches, that the kind of ethical education proposed in this volume is indeed possible.
BECKER, E. (1967) *Beyond Alienation: A Philosophy of Education for the Crisis of Democracy*, New York, George Braziller; BECKER, E. (1968) *The Structure of Evil: An Essay on the Unification of the Science of Man*, New York, Free Press.
In both of these books, Becker contends that children are socialized to

surrender their freedom and autonomy to their parents and then to other authorities, like teachers, who teach them to subject their freedom and autonomy to further strictures in the form of the conventions of culture. Becker challenges the schools to help youngsters overcome the alienation and anxiety that results from their socialization process. His proposals contain many similarities to those proposed in my chapter on the ideal ethical school. Becker is a challenging writer because his scholarship casts such a broad net across the waters of philosophy, sociology, psychology and anthropology. However, he provides a firm intellectual foundation for those seeking to build an ethical school.

BELLAH, R., MADSEN, R. SULLIVAN, W., SWIDLER, A. and TIPTON, S. (1985) *Habits of the Heart*, Berkeley, University of California Press; BELLAH, R., MADSEN, R., SULLIVAN, W., SWIDLER, A. and TIPTON, S. (1991) *The Good Society*, New York, Alfred A. Knopf.

Bellah and his associates have provided an appealing commentary on the dangers of an excessive concentration on the individual and on individual happiness as dangers to American public life. Their detailed description of how this individualism gets played out both in small town and urban life by professionals and clerical workers alike indicates a serious erosion in people's faith in public institutions and in their confidence that they could change things in public life. Bellah and his associates' work provides a foundation for Chapters 2 and 3 of this book and provides interesting reading for teachers and administrators involved in building an ethical school. In one sense, the attempt to build an ethical school is a direct response to the dangers highlighted in their books.

BOTTERY, M. (1990) *The Morality of the School: The Theory and Practice of Values in Education*, London, Cassell.

This book is an interesting marriage of theoretical perspectives and practical suggestions for dealing with values in education. Writing from a British perspective, Bottery summarizes enormous bodies of ethical literature well. His charts and tables enable a quick review of major figures in the field of moral education. His practical suggestions for curriculum development should prove stimulating to teachers at all levels. His seven appendices contain many specific exercises for developing moral reasoning and ethical attitudes.

BOULDING, E. (1988) *Building a Global Civic Culture*, New York, Teachers College Press.

Boulding, long considered a mature voice in global education, has gathered the insights from her many years of travel, study and conversation with international scholars, educators and leaders of governmental and non-governmental efforts in international development into a compelling argument for expanding our social imaginations to build a more peaceful and interconnected world. Boulding argues for the integration of thinking, feeling and acting in remaking ourselves and our world into a more peaceful place. She goes beyond platitudes in offering serious analyses of the uses of the imagination in imagining a global future, in exploring the effectiveness of international non-governmental organizations and the networks of effective action they have created, and in digging beneath ethnic, racial and religious diversity to 'species identity'. The book is a storehouse of ideas for those concerned with the ethics of international and cultural relations in the global village.

BRICKER, D. (1989) *Classroom Life as Civic Education*, New York, Teachers College Press.

Bricker exposes an underlying philosophy of ethics, based on a philosophy of the person, and the person's relationship to society, in the thinking of teachers. This underlying philosophy is the classical liberal philosophy, namely that the individual — and not the family, the community, or the state — is the basic unit of society. His book illustrates how teachers unreflectingly act out this philosophy in the classroom, and thus communicate and socialize students into this definition of reality. He goes on to argue for a necessary counterbalance to this liberal philosophy, namely, a philosophy of communitarianism. The argument in this book would illuminate why I chose to include the ethic of care with the ethic of justice in the chapter on ethical frameworks. This book would be a challenging, but important reading for teachers who want to build an ethical school.

BRYK, A. (1988) 'Musings on the moral life of schools', *American Journal of Education*, **96**, February, pp. 256–90.

This issue of the *AJE* is entirely devoted to the topic of moral education. Bryk's essay provides a good commentary on the other essays in the issue and raises probing questions about the possibilities for an enriched ethical education within schools with a strong sense of community. His thinking would be reflected in the chapter on the ideal ethical school.

CARR, D. (1991) *Educating the Virtues*, London, Routledge.

This book delineates central philosophical schools of thought on ethical education with Plato, Aristotle, Rousseau and Kant. The author believes, and I tend to agree with him, that these four have laid out the basic map of positions on the subject. Those who follow them can be seen as developers of one or another of the four positions established by these writers. He goes on to discuss developments in conceptions of ethical education influenced by four scholars in the social sciences, namely, Durkheim, Freud, Piaget and Kohlberg. The early part of the book lays the groundwork for the author's own theory of the virtues, which is developed basically within the Aristotelian framework. The author writes with Scottish rigor and felicity. I would not suggest this as the initial book for the uninitiated, although I would not have included it in this bibliography if I did not find it a very helpful contribution to the clarification of our thinking about ethical education.

CARTER, R. (1984) *Dimensions of Moral Education*, Toronto, University of Toronto Press.

For the more philosophically minded, this book provides a critical analysis of various theories of ethics, from Plato, to Kohlberg, to the Existentialists, to the Linguistic Analysts. The author plants himself, in the final chapter, in an ethics of the person, synthesizing perspectives from Macmurray, Cassirer, Hartman and Camus. His last chapter supports much of what I have proposed in the development of foundational qualities. Though challenging, this is good stuff for inquiring minds.

COLES, R. (1989) *The Call of Stories: Teaching and the Moral Imagination*, Boston, Houghton Mifflin Company.

Robert Coles, one of the most engaging scholars of our time, reflects on the power of stories to engage our moral sensibilities. His book suggests the strong influence which stories can have in our education of the young.

COUSINEAU, P. (Ed.) (1990) *The Hero's Journey: Joseph Campbell on His Life and Work*, San Francisco, Harper & Row.

This book presents Joseph Campbell commenting on his writings, especially on his work, *The Hero With a Thousand Faces*. His commentary illuminates the heroic journey of everyman, as it is reflected in the myths of various cultures. Campbell's work reinforces my development of the notion of transcendence in the chapter on foundational qualities.

CRAFT, A. and BARDELL, G. (Eds) (1984) *Curriculum Opportunities in a Multicultural Society*, London: Harper & Row.

Developed as a result of their involvement in the project, 'Assessment in a Multicultural Society', for the British Schools Council, this book contains insightful essays by a variety of British educators on the integration of multicultural perspectives within traditional curriculum areas such as Mathematics, Science, Humanities,

Language and Literature and the Arts. Besides the expected use of multicultural material in the humanities and the arts, the book contains many interesting examples of dealing with what I have called foundational qualities or pre-ethical dispositions in other academic disciplines as well. Observing how educators in a previously monocultural society are dealing with diversity can be instructive indeed for those of us who consider ourselves knowledgeable about multicultural education.

ELIAS, J. (1989) *Moral Education/Secular and Religious.* Malabar, FL, Robert E. Krieger Publishing Company.

This is a comprehensive overview of various points of view about moral education (philosophical, psychological, sociological and theological). His introduction to the book points out many subtle tensions to be found in moral education, tensions between individual moral choices and the larger social good, between reason and affect, between the content and the form of moral education, and between freedom and responsibility to others. A solid, scholarly work.

ELKIND, D. (1984) *All Grown Up and No Place to Go*, Reading, MA, Addison-Wesley Publishing Company.

A good overview of adolescence, its crises and ways for adults to help.

FEINBERG, W. (1990) 'The moral responsibility of the public schools', in GOODLAD, J., SODER, R. and SIROTNIK, K.A. (Eds) *The Moral Dimension of Teaching*, San Francisco, Jossey-Bass, pp. 155–87.

This is an excellent essay on the responsibility of public schools to provide moral education for its students. Feinberg argues the need for moral citizens who are committed to the public good and to the public-forming debate on public policy — in short, to the moral values of democracy.

FOX, R.M. and DEMARCO, J.P. (1990) *Moral Reasoning: A Philosophical Approach to Applied Ethics*, Fort Worth, TX, Holt, Rinehart & Winston, Inc.

The authors provide a good overview of moral reasoning, the major ethical theories, and the development and application of a set of moral principles.

FRAZER, M.J. and KORNHAUSER, A. (1986) *Ethics and Social Responsibility in Science Education*, New York, Pergamon Press.

This is one of a series of volumes commissioned by the Committee on the Teaching of Science of the International Council of Scientific Unions (ICSU). The book contains brief essays by international scholars on scientific issues such as chemical pollution, tissue transplants, food production and distribution, as well as essays on pedagogical methodology, providing a rich source of ideas for science teachers at all grade levels.

FROMM, E. (1947) *Man for Himself: An Inquiry into the Psychology of Ethics*, New York, Fawcett Premier Books.

Fromm provides an insightful foundation for a humanistic ethics, one which is based on productive love and productive thinking. The main production for human beings is themselves, individually and collectively, precisely as humans. To this productive orientation he contrasts various non-productive orientations which are commonly found in communities of people.

GARDNER, J.W. (1961) *Excellence: Can We Be Equal and Excellent Too?* New York, Harper & Row; GARDNER, J.W. (1963) *Self-Renewal: The Individual and the Innovative Society*, New York, Harper & Row.

These two books remain a classic commentary on the pursuit of excellence and self-governance. The excellence theme relates especially to the foundational qualities of autonomy and transcendence. The self-renewal theme relates to the very process of building an ethical school. That process is one of self-renewal, and Gardiner instructs us wisely about the challenges of that process.

GOODLAD, J., SODER, R. and SIROTNIK, K. (Eds) (1990) *The Moral Dimensions of Teaching*, San Francisco, Jossey-Bass.

This book contains thoughtful essays by recognized scholars in the field of education, and has helped to rekindle interest in the ethical dimensions of teaching.

GROSS, R. and DYNNESON, T. (Eds) (1991) *Social Science Perspectives on Citizenship Education*, New York, Teachers College Press.

The editors have gathered an impressive series of ten essays on citizenship education from various social science perspectives. This volume would be valuable for social studies teachers and departments seeking to raise social justice questions in their courses and seeking to encourage positive attitudes about citizen involvement in public life among their students.

HENNESSY, T. (Ed.) (1976) *Values and Moral Development*, New York, Paulist Press; HENNESSY, T. (Ed.) (1979) *Value/Moral Education: Schools and Teachers*, New York, Paulist Press.

The first of these volumes brings together succinct theoretical presentations of some of the best North American thinkers on moral and ethical education (Beck, Sprinthall, Sullivan, Rest, Selman, Havighurst and Fowler) along with critical responses to their positions by other educators. The second volume presents a fascinating collection of essays by some of the best teachers of moral education, and concludes with an interview of Lawrence Kohlberg.

Together these volumes contain a gold mine of ideas and perspectives for anyone exploring the field of ethical education.

HESCHEL, A. (1963) *Who Is Man?* Stanford, CA, Stanford University Press.

A compilation of lectures given at Stanford University, this small book captures the essential humanism of a marvelously humane scholar. This book helped to provide the fundamental perspectives developed in Chapter 3. Though he obviously brings in his Hebrew biblical understanding, his book is not about God, but about human beings. To illustrate the pithy, poetic prose so abundantly flowing in this book: 'Ontology inquires: What is Being? Epistemology enquires: What is thinking? The heart of man inquires: What is expected of me?' This leads us toward ethical living.

LEICESTER, M. and TAYLOR, M. (Eds) (1992) *Ethics, Ethnicity and Education*, London, Kogan Page.

This collection of essays by British educators moves beyond the debate over the distinction between multicultural and antiracist education. The authors recognize racism in their society and write from an ethical commitment to oppose it. The essays encompass theoretical explorations about how to educate morally in a democratic pluralist society, as well as reports of empirical research of students' and teachers' racist sentiments in their schools. The book is written in response to the Education Acts of 1986 and 1988 in England and Wales, which appear to move those countries in inegalitarian directions in a society that is already riven by racism. As with other books written outside the US borders, it is instructive to consider our own social situation from the vantage point of others' perspectives, especially when they are so articulately presented.

LEMING, J.S. (1983) *Contemporary Approaches to Moral Education: An Annotated Bibliography and Guide to Research*, New York, Garland Publishing.

This book contains a gold mine of references to works dealing with ethical education, from the theoretical to the practical. There are many fine references to material that deals with ethics in subject matter content areas such as science, literature and social studies.

LEONARD LAMME, L., LOWELL KROUGH, S. and YACHMETZ, K. (1992) *Literature Based Moral Education*, Phoenix, AZ, Oryx Press.

This idea-packed little book promotes nine values: self esteem, responsibility, sharing, truthfulness, solving conflicts peacefully, respecting others, valuing the environment, diligence, unconditional love. A chapter is devoted to the teaching of each of these values through literature, and recommended readings for the students are to be found at the end of each chapter. For language arts teachers, this is a treasure-trove of ideas and sources. Must reading!

LICKONA, T. (1989) *Education for Character*, New York, Bantam Books.
From one of the outstanding scholars in the field of moral education comes a comprehensive survey of up-to-date information on moral education. Lickona's book is chock-full of practical ideas garnered from schools across the country. This would be most helpful for teachers in grades one through eight, although high school teachers would benefit from the book as well. Many of the sources for materials in Appendix I were found in this book.

LYNCH, J. (1992) *Education for Citizenship in a Multi-Cultural Society*, London, Cassell.
Lynch, an educational consultant to the World Bank, brings a wealth of international source material to his proposals for citizenship education. His concerns cover citizenship at the local, national and international level; one cannot educate a citizen for only one or two of these levels because the present and future reality involves the interpenetration of all three. Lynch clearly sees education for citizenship, embracing, beyond knowledge and technical problem-solving skills, ethical principles and value priorities. His book moves from a broad rationale for citizenship education, to a consideration of policies and systemic processes, to school and classroom practice. A tightly written book, it requires careful reading to mine the riches it contains. It provides a good source of ideas on the connectedness theme as well as the integration of the three frameworks of justice, care and critique. This is the best book on citizenship education I have read.

MACINTYRE, A. (1984) *After Virtue*, 2nd Edn, Notre Dame, IN, Notre Dame University Press.
This historical analysis of a philosophical basis for morality has generated both controversy and acclaim. Many educators, not well versed in philosophy, might find it tedious, if not excessively abstract and pedantically argumentative. Nonetheless, for the stout-hearted, a wrestle with this book will sharpen one's own position, and develop an historical depth to one's knowledge of ethical theory. Carr's work, mentioned above, covers much of the same ground, and in my judgment, more felicitously. MacIntyre would challenge the methodology behind our effort to build an ethical school as not being philosophically rigorous enough. My response is that, although he may be correct philosophically, to follow his advice would leave us with a school for a very select community of

believers around his ideas. My project to build ethical schools which embrace the very diversity of their students as the stuff out of which ethical choices are forged would have to be put aside.

MAGUIRE, D. and FARGNOLI, A.N. (1991) *On Moral Grounds: The Art/ Science of Ethics*, New York, Crossroad.

This book speaks intelligently about moral experience, about ethics as 'the strategy of justice and love', explores routes to moral truth, and clarifies the meaning of conscience. The authors present a clear distinction between an ethic of justice and an ethic of friendship, yet show how both are needed. This book offers support for the foundational qualities of autonomy, connectedness and transcendence. The authors ground their whole presentation of morality on a foundational moral experience — the experience of the value of persons and their environment.

MCLEAN, G., ELROD, F., SCHINDLER, D. and MANN, J. (Eds) (1986) *Act and Agent: Philosophical Foundations for Moral Education and Character Development*, Lanham, MD, University Press of America.

This is a good source book for philosophical considerations of the moral agent. The essays in the book circle around the theme of moral autonomy.

NUCCI, L. (Ed.) (1989) *Moral Development and Character Education: A Dialogue*, Berkeley, CA, McCutchan Publishing Corporation.

This book contains sets of essays by the character education school and by the cognitive developmental school of ethical education. The former tends to favor overt socialization into traditional virtues while the latter tends to socialize youngsters into dialogic ways of solving moral problems. A third group, however, manages to sneak into the conversation and they seem to present the most appealing approach to moral education, which is a mixture of social learning theory, derived from Albert Bandura, and cognitive developmental theory derived from Piaget and Kohlberg. They describe the Child Development Project, a longitudinal program focused on the prosocial development of elementary school children in three schools in a middle-class suburban community in northern California. While the program is described in very clear and appealing detail in the fourth chapter of this book, a more detailed discussion of the program may be found in the essay by Hector Battistich and colleagues (1990), 'The child development project: A comprehensive program for the development of prosocial character', in KURTINES, W. and GEWIRTZ, J. (Eds) *Moral Development and Behavior: Advances in Theory, Research and Application*, Vol. I, Hillsdale, NJ, Erlbaum. Nucci includes an insightful essay by Nona Lyons on the logic of the ethic of caring, as well as his own concluding essay in which he presents a helpful distinction between social convention and universal moral concerns. His book presents a fine overview of the points of view one would expect to encounter in a community attempting to build an ethical school. I strongly recommend this book.

PALMER, P. (1985) *The Company of Strangers*, New York, Crossroad.

The author, an educator and a Quaker writer on spirituality, writes eloquently about the need to renew public life in the USA with an insightful universality. His themes intersect nicely with the foundational qualities of autonomy, connectedness and transcendence.

PEARSON, C. (1989) *The Hero Within: Six Archetypes We Live By*, New York, Harper & Row.

In her search for feminine heroes in American and British literature, Pearson found that women changed the male version of the hero story — from the hero-kills-the-villain-and-rescues-the-victim plot, to a plot with no real villains or victims, just heroes. She traces the journey humans take through adopting successive hero archetypes. The book is instructive for conceptualizing forms which the foundational qualities of autonomy and transcendence might take.

PETERSON, R. (1992) *Life in a Crowded Place: Making a Learning Community*, Portsmouth, NH, Heinemann.

Peterson, a veteran teacher himself, offers helpful, practical suggestions for teachers seeking to explore a more holistic approach to their teaching, an approach that includes building community among students, and using the life experience of the student community as a valuable part of the curriculum. Many of this examples would be located comfortably in our description of our ideal ethical school.

POPKEWITZ, T.S. (1992) *A Political Sociology of Educational Reform*, New York, Teachers College Press.

This book is not for the faint-hearted. I include it because it is an excellent example of someone writing from a foundation of the ethic of critique about how schools and school curriculum reflect the dominant ideologies of their times. These ideological positions, whether about the nature of scientific knowledge or about the social purposes of schooling, become incorporated into ways of thinking about and into the definitions of reality found in school textbooks and in school organizational patterns. The book assumes some knowledge of contemporary philosophy and its debates, so it will be beyond the comprehension of most people without such a background, unfortunately. I say 'unfortunately' because it is a first rate work, one that provides a strong foundation for the careful reconstruction of schooling.

PURPEL, D. (1989) *The Moral and Spiritual Crisis in Education*, Granby, MA, Bergin & Garvey.

The author describes the conflicts in American culture which are reproduced as conflicts in the schools. He goes on to propose a religious framework that is not anchored in any specific religious institution or orthodoxy, but instead is grounded in a common emotion or conviction that there is some transcendent source of meaning and life which sanctifies and makes the world real. He goes on to propose a curriculum for social justice and compassion. The book is brimming with foundational ideas and would provide stimulating reading for teachers who are exploring curriculum ideas for ethical education.

RYAN, K. and McLEAN, G. (Eds) (1987) *Character Development in Schools and Beyond*, New York, Praeger.

The book contains essays by many who have been identified with the character education school, but also contains essays by others who do not fit comfortably into that descriptor (myself included). In the first chapter, Kevin Ryan and Thomas Lickona present a helpful model of the moral agent, exploring the cognitive, affective and behavioral components of the moral agent's development. In part three, there are chapters detailing possibilities for ethical education in the elementary, junior high and senior high school. Part four explores the effects of family, religion and the media (especially television) on the ethical development of young people. A good sourcebook with a variety of perspectives.

SCHARF, P. (1978) *Moral Education*, Davis, CA, Responsible Action.

The author has worked closely with Lawrence Kohlberg, and his book develops many of the themes initiated by Kohlberg. After introductory chapters developed to highlight Kohlberg's theory of moral development, Scharf presents several helpful chapters in which he reviews classroom treatments of moral issues within core curriculum subjects such as literature, social studies, natural sciences and physical education. One chapter contains an insightful treatment of the school as a place for nurturing democratic values and practices.

STARRATT, R. (1990) *The Drama of Schooling/The Schooling of Drama*, London, Falmer Press.

While not precisely a book on moral education, the book develops ideas related to the foundational qualities of autonomy, connectedness and transcendence. These ideas are developed through and around metaphors of drama.

STOCK MORTON, P. (1988) *Moral Education for a Secular Society*, Albany, NY, State University of New York Press.

In a fascinating historical study, the author traces the contentious development in France of *morale laïque*, from its roots in the Enlightenment to its gradual obsolescence as a perfunctory part of the curriculum of state schools in twentieth-century France. France was the European country most intent on establishing a moral education independent of the Church. During the nineteenth century, some of the best philosophical minds in France attempted to develop a secular philosophical foundation for morality. Ironically, Durkheim's philosophical system is acknowledged by most philosophers to have grounded secular moral education most adequately, but it was rejected by most of his countrymen, as not allowing enough freedom for the individual — an unforgivable defect in a culture which so cherishes the individual. While this book would not be recommended for most, due to its concentration on French history, the issues it treats — the possibility of a secular morality not grounded in religion — remain among the most contentious issues facing educators who would build an ethical school within the state or educational system.

TAYLOR, C. (1991) *The Ethics of Authenticity*, Cambridge, MA, Harvard University Press.

I came across this volume after the manuscript for this book was pretty well complete, and wish I had found it earlier. Taylor, a well respected contemporary philosopher, elaborates on the meaning of authenticity in much the same way I do on autonomy, but he does it better. As with any philosophical writing, those not familiar with this genre will find it difficult; Taylor, however, writes with greater lucidity than most philosophers and, in the case of this book, much more succinctly. His ancillary treatments of two other contemporary themes, namely, the limitations of instrumental reasoning, and the weakening of political intelligence and will in the public sphere, would also resonate with themes I have taken up in the chapter on the moral problematics of schooling. This book will be very helpful for those trying to develop the foundational qualities for ethical education.

THOMAS, B. (1990) 'The school as a moral learning community', in GOODLAD, J., SODER, R. and SIROTNIK, K. (Eds) *The Moral Dimensions of Teaching*, San Francisco, Jossey Bass, pp. 266–95.

In this essay Thomas highlights the lessons of the famous Eight Year

Study. In that study American educators and their communities conducted an intensive and extensive study of what schools which took democracy seriously might look like. They discovered that it was possible to pursue democratic social organization and autonomous moral growth at the same time. This essay, coupled with Aiken's report of the Eight Year Study provides ample evidence that an effort to build an ethical school within the public school system is indeed possible.

WHITE, J. (1991) *Education and the Good Life: Autonomy, Altruism, and the National Curriculum*, New York, Teachers College Press.

The author, a professor of education in England (Institute of Education, University of London), criticizes the National Curriculum mandated in 1988 for English and Welsh schools. Lost amidst the list of objectives is any sense of the aim of the whole enterprise, charges White. He proposes that one of the central aims of education should be the development of moral persons. He urges that schools avoid the endless arguments over 'whose morality' should be taught, by substituting 'education in altruism' for the idea of moral education. He offers a rather benign list of altruistic dispositions, with which few would argue, and which could serve those trying to build an ethical school. His treatment of autonomy bears similarities to my own treatment of that foundational quality, although he tends to stress the isolated individual as the source of moral decisions, rather than continuously placing the individual in a social context of other persons whose interests influence the choices of the individual and vice versa. The book provides yet another example of educators attempting to go beyond the technical academic agenda to a larger view of an education of more complete persons.

Index

NATIONAL UNIVERSITY
LIBRARY   SAN DIEGO

5313